# Caring for someone who is dying

## Penny Mares

**AGE** *Concern*

BOOKS

© 1994 Penny Mares
**Published by Age Concern England**
1268 London Road
London SW16 4ER

First published 1994 in Age Concern Books' *Caring in a Crisis* series
This edition published 1998

Editor  Caroline Hartnell
Production  Vinnette Marshall
Designed and typeset by  GreenGate Publishing Services, Tonbridge, Kent
Printed in Great Britain by Bell & Bain Ltd, Glasgow

A catalogue record for this book is available from the British Library.

ISBN 0-86242-260-4

**Bulk orders**

Age Concern England is pleased to offer customised editions of all its titles to UK
companies, institutions or other organisations wishing to make a bulk purchase.
For further information, please contact the Publishing Department at the address
above. Tel: 0181-679 8000. Fax: 0181-679 6069. E-mail: addisom@ace.org.uk.

# Contents

# About the author

Penny Mares is an established writer on health issues. She has written a range of information and training materials for people caring at home. She is author of *You and Caring* published by the King's Fund and co-author of *Who Cares Now?*, the book which accompanies the BBC *Who Cares Now?* TV series on caring for an older person.

# Acknowledgements

For their helpful comments on what should go into this book I should like to thank Judy Fitton, Carers National Association (Leeds), especially for her idea of the jigsaw puzzle; the Macmillan nurses, Kirkstall health centre; Dr Dawn Allison and Lorna Foyle, Macmillan nurse, Palliative Care Team, St James's Hospital; Maureen Wilson, Principal Social Worker, Wheatfields Hospice; Cecile Levine, Welfare Benefits Adviser, Bradford Cancer Support Centre; and Drs Sally and Adrian Stanley, general practitioners.

I should especially like to thank the carers who talked to me about their own experiences of caring for someone with a terminal illness. Their stories are the basis of the case studies and quotes which appear throughout the book. The case studies are not 'real' in that names and details have been altered, but they are based on real events.

I am grateful for permission to adapt material from the following publications: *What to do and who to turn to* by Marina Lewycka (Age Concern Books, 1994), *Facing the Challenge of Advanced Cancer* (BACUP, 1992), *You and Caring* by Penny Mares (King's Fund, 1992) and *Who Cares Now? Caring for an older person* by Nancy Kohner and Penny Mares (BBC Education, 1991). The charts on pages 27–30 are adapted from *Caring at Home When Cancer Cannot Be Cured* (Cancerlink, 1993). The extract on pages 54–55 is the copyright of Dr Robert Buckman and is reproduced from *I Don't Know What to Say* (Papermac, 1988, pp 60–61) by kind permission of Macmillan, London. The 'grief work' diagram on page 92 is adapted from *Facing Death* by Averil Stedeford (Heinemann Medical, 1984, p 153).

# Introduction

Are you caring at home for a friend or relative who has a terminal illness? Or looking after someone who lives nearby? Or trying to organise care and support at a distance – perhaps for a parent? If you are, then this book is designed to help you through some of the difficulties that you and the person you look after may face in the days ahead.

Terminal illness is not easy to define. With any illness, no one can predict exactly what will happen. The information in this book will be most helpful to people who are caring for someone who is in the later stages of an illness which cannot be cured – for example, cancer which has come back, or which is in an advanced stage, or the final stages of a disease such as multiple sclerosis, motor neurone disease, AIDS, chronic heart disease or chronic chest disease. Or it may be that the person you look after does not have a specific disease, but is simply old and very frail and is thought unlikely to live much longer.

The person needing care may be a spouse or partner, a parent, sibling or another relative, or a close friend. For simplicity we refer to 'your relative' throughout the book, and 'she' and 'he' in alternate chapters.

## How to use this book

Organising the help and support that you need to help you care for someone who is dying is in some ways like trying to do a jigsaw puzzle. No one can predict what is going to happen, and everyone involved has to live with uncertainty – for each person the puzzle fits together in a unique way.

This book aims to help you sort out what you need to help you care and to fit the parts of the puzzle together in the way that makes most sense to you. It takes you through all the stages of caring for someone with a terminal illness.

Chapter 1 starts with the diagnosis itself, and the feelings of both ill person and carer on hearing the news. Chapter 2 deals with finding out more about the illness, and Chapter 3 looks at the various sorts of help you might be able to get if you decide to care for your relative at home. Chapter 4 deals with money matters – getting help with the costs of caring, taking over your relative's affairs if necessary, and the things your relative might want to do to put her affairs in order.

Chapter 5 then looks at the middle stages of the illness, which might last for anything from a few weeks to a few years, and Chapter 6 moves on to the stage when death is near. Chapter 7 covers the practical things that need to be done after someone has died, while Chapter 8 talks about coping with bereavement and grief.

When you pick up this book, the person you care for may have only recently learned that she is dying, or may have known for some time, or may not know at all. The illness may be in the early stages, or it may be fairly advanced.

You may be looking for ideas and information about the practical side of caring. You may be wanting to talk to your friend or relative about what is happening, but wondering what on earth you can say.

Where you start reading will depend on which part of the jigsaw is most important for you at the time. Later you might want to go forwards or backwards to fit the other parts of the puzzle together.

Caring for someone who is dying is a sad and difficult thing to do. If this book helps you to find some way, however small, to make things better than they would otherwise have been, it will have served its purpose.

> *With what strife and pains we come into the world we*
> *know not, but 'tis commonly no easy matter to get out*
> *of it*          Thomas Browne, *Religio Medici*, 1643.

# 1 The diagnosis

*Learning that you have an illness that cannot be cured is devastating. Each person has to find their own way of coping with what is probably the most frightening and lonely situation that they have ever faced. Often the ill person's partner, relative or close friend feels lonely and frightened too.*

*Everyone's feelings and experience are different, but this chapter describes some of the common reactions that people – and their carers – go through on learning that they have a terminal illness. Understanding these reactions may help you to provide the support and help that your relative needs to face the future.*

*Sometimes it is left to the carer to decide whether the person who is ill should be told, or to decide who else should be told and how. The last part of this chapter discusses these difficult situations.*

## Celia

'I couldn't believe it. I couldn't take in what he had said, and I couldn't believe the way he had done it.'

'Martin had been told that he was suffering from a disorder of the white blood cells that was fairly common in older people. We were both stunned when the consultant told us one day that his condition seemed to be deteriorating, and there was a possibility that it might develop into full-blown leukaemia. The worst part was that the consultant said he couldn't predict if or when it would happen.

'Martin had to keep going backwards and forwards to the hospital for blood transfusions and tests to see what was happening. I arrived one morning to collect him after an overnight stay for a blood transfusion to find him in tears. The consultant had visited him and told him that it had become full-blown leukaemia, and that he needed chemotherapy as soon as possible or he would be dead within three months. I couldn't believe it. I couldn't take in what he had said, and I couldn't believe the way he had done it. I felt so angry that he couldn't have waited and told us together. Martin had just crumpled and I had no idea what to do – I was as shattered as he was.'

# Feelings on learning the diagnosis

Like Martin, many people learn that they have a terminal illness from a doctor, often at a stage when they are still feeling quite healthy, or only a little under the weather. But whatever stage the illness has reached, the ill person often regards herself as basically healthy or ill-but-going-to-get-better. Suddenly she has to face the idea that she is going to die.

People react to this crisis in different ways. They vary in how much time they need to absorb the diagnosis, and in how much information they are able to take in at once. But there is a pattern in the way people tend to react. Understanding this pattern may help you to make sense of what your relative is going through, and give you insight into your own reactions and feelings.

## Shock and disbelief

Martin and Celia's first reaction was one of shock and disbelief. This is a very normal response. The person who is ill, and the carer too, may feel as though they are cut off from the rest of the world and find it hard to take anything in. People often say things like 'I can't believe this is happening to me' or 'I keep hoping I'll wake up and find it's all a dream'. Outwardly people sometimes seem to slow down and find it difficult to concentrate, while inwardly their feelings may be in turmoil. At first feelings of disbelief may come and go, as though the brain needs to keep re-running the idea before it can sink in. This period may last for hours or days, or sometimes even longer.

## *Denial*

After the initial shock there is often a tendency for both the ill person and her carer to try and play down or ignore the seriousness of the crisis. This seems to be a natural defence mechanism which helps to prevent us feeling completely overwhelmed, and gives us time to come to terms with what is happening. The term 'denial' covers a range of reactions, but in the end these boil down to 'I won't accept this'. These are the sorts of things that people often say:

- 'They must have made a mistake with the test results.'
- 'I don't think the doctor knows what he's doing – I want to get a second opinion.'
- 'I feel all right, so it can't be as bad as they make out.'
- 'If it's bad news I don't want to hear about it.'
- 'It can't be so serious – we've already planned our holiday for next year.'

The denial phase may last from days to weeks or months. Some people never move beyond this phase.

## *Anger and grief*

As the ill person begins to accept the diagnosis, denial often gives way to feelings of anger about what is happening. Sometimes the ill person's anger is directed at the doctor who bears the bad news or at the person giving care. People also feel a sense of grief for what is being lost. The ill person may look back at the time when she was healthy, and mourn for the loss of her past life.

Carers may experience feelings similar to those of the ill person. Sometimes, along with grief at the impending loss of the person they love, carers may also feel guilt that they might have contributed to the illness in some way, and anger at themselves, or at the person who is ill (because in some ways they feel let down or stranded by the illness). Often there are also feelings of guilt or relief – or both at once – that it is not they who have the illness. All these reactions are natural.

## *Fear*

Most people are afraid at some point during a serious illness – afraid of the illness, afraid of dying, afraid about what will happen to their partner or family after they die. Perhaps more than anything else, people with a terminal illness need someone who is prepared to listen and talk to them about their feelings and fears. Carers, too, may feel fearful about the future and about how they will cope when the ill person has died.

## *Other feelings*

These are some of the feelings that you and the person you care for may have in the period after learning the diagnosis. As she begins to adjust to the illness, these may give way to different emotions – feelings of depression and isolation are common in the middle stages. Towards the end of their illness, some people are able to come to terms with and sometimes calmly accept the fact of approaching death, but others never reach acceptance.

All these feelings – and others – may recur during a long illness. Each time there is a deterioration or an increase in disability, both the ill person and the person who is caring have to make a new adjustment and come to terms with new limitations.

## Maureen

'You think you're dealing with it, and that you're prepared for what's going to happen, and then there's a change – my husband seemed to be doing all right, and then he started to get very confused and sometimes he was hallucinating with the drugs – and it's as though you have to start climbing a mountain all over again.'

# What can you do to help?

The diagnosis of terminal illness leaves us feeling powerless because it is something beyond our control. The following list suggests some concrete things you can do to help and support the person you care for and to help both of you to feel less powerless and more in control. Some of these are adapted from useful guidelines offered by Dr Robert Buckman in his book *I Don't Know What to Say*.

- Accept your relative's feelings, and be prepared for her to want to go over the same ground again and again. Be prepared, too, for sharp swings in mood and outlook. This is part of the process of coming to terms with what is happening.
- Recognise your own feelings. Try and sort out the feelings that are helpful from the ones that are not so helpful.
- Encourage your relative to talk about her feelings, and try to be open and honest about your own. You may find it hard to know what to say – most people do – but just showing that you *want* to listen and understand is a way of giving support.
- If you find it very difficult to talk openly to each other, encourage your relative to find someone she can open up to – perhaps another member of the family, a friend, or a doctor or nurse.
- Encourage your relative to draw on the strength of her own past experience, to think back to difficult and threatening situations that she has coped with and to use this strength to face the illness.

■ Work out how you can help most. Avoid the temptation to rush in and take over with help that you can't keep up in the long term.

■ Let your relative make the decisions, don't make them for her. Find out what she wants to do. Let her take the lead in deciding what support she wants.

■ Being there may be more important than doing things. Rushing around may help you to feel better, but your relative might rather have your company for a couple of hours.

■ Get more information. People who are under a great deal of stress find it very difficult to take in information. You can help your relative to understand her illness, to ask questions when she wants to know more, and to make informed decisions about treatment or care.

## For more *i*nformation

ℹ *I Don't Know What to Say: How to help and support someone who is dying* by Robert Buckman, published by Papermac. This sympathetic and easy-to-read book is written for the family and friends of people facing a terminal illness. It is now out of print but worth getting hold of through your public library.

ℹ See pages 66–67 for more about feelings in the middle stages of illness.

ℹ Some common fears about dying are discussed on pages 71–75.

# Does the ill person need to know?

Sometimes the person who is ill is not told the full diagnosis by the doctor. It may be left to a relative or close friend to decide whether or how much she should be told. This can be a very difficult decision. The simple answer is that it is up to the ill person to decide how much she wants to know. Every situation is different, but these are some of the factors you may want to think about:

■ Sometimes the person giving care doesn't want the ill person to know in order to protect her, but not telling often puts a huge strain on the relationship.

■ Research studies show that most people want to know the truth, and that people who feel fully informed tend to cope better than those who don't.

■ Your relative may not want to hear the whole story all at once. She may need time to take in the diagnosis and to reach a point where she wants to know more. Let her set the pace.

■ Your relative may make it clear that she doesn't want to know. If not knowing is not causing any distress, there may be no reason to tell her. People who don't want to know often ignore what they are told, or filter out the parts they don't want to hear.

■ If your relative is getting more and more anxious about the illness and uncertainty, she will probably cope better if she is told the full diagnosis.

■ Having someone who will listen and talk openly with her about her feelings makes it easier for a sick person to come to terms with her illness.

■ Generally professionals will not lie to a patient. If other family members ask a doctor or nurse not to tell the sick person the whole truth, they might agree not to volunteer information that the person is not ready to hear. But they may also say that if they are asked a direct question they will give an honest answer.

# Who else should be told?

People vary in what they decide to tell other relatives and friends about a terminal illness. It is often helpful to be open with other people, and to encourage them to be open with the person who is ill. Not telling other people can leave the sick person feeling very isolated, and puts a lot of strain on the carer.

It is natural to want to protect children, but not telling them about the illness can leave them feeling excluded or frightened because they sense that something is wrong but don't know what. Deciding how and what to tell them will depend on their age and how much they can understand, but even very young children can understand a simple explanation.

Some people may find it very difficult to talk about the illness but genuinely want to help in other ways. Some people may feel so frightened by the illness that they avoid contact altogether. People who react like this do so because of their own fear, but it can be very hurtful for the ill person and the carer. It may be easier to accept there is nothing you can do about this than to try and keep in contact.

# 2 Understanding the illness

*As you and your relative begin to come to terms with the fact that his illness cannot be cured, you will both probably want to know a lot more about what is likely to happen in the weeks and months ahead. This chapter sets out some questions that you or your relative may want to ask and some decisions you may need to consider.*

*Patients and carers often feel they are not given enough information about the illness and treatment. This chapter also suggests ways of tackling this difficulty and some helpful sources of information.*

## Parveen

'We found ourselves starting to ask all sorts of questions, and it seemed as though we never got straight answers.'

'As the fact of my mother's illness began to sink in, we found ourselves starting to ask all sorts of questions, and it seemed as though we never got straight answers. The consultant was telling us things which sometimes didn't make sense, or which seemed to contradict what the GP was saying.

'The worst thing was that the consultant was a very brusque, unapproachable woman, and the other doctors we saw kept saying they couldn't tell us anything, we would have to ask her. I mentioned to a staff nurse how difficult it was to get information out of any of the doctors, and she said I ought to phone the consultant's secretary and make an appointment to see her. It's something I would never have thought of doing myself – I was actually a bit scared of her – but it was very useful. She told me a lot about the treatment and possible side-effects and generally what to be prepared for in the months ahead.'

# How to find out about the illness

If no one tells you anything, your imagination has to fill in the gaps. Most people with a terminal illness feel very vulnerable and frightened, and often the people who are caring for them do too. Information can reduce fear and enable people to feel more in control.

Patients and carers also need information in order to make all sorts of decisions – about where the ill person can best be cared for, about what sort of care and support is needed and who is going to provide it, about financial arrangements, and perhaps even about things like whether to go on holiday or move house. Without enough information, it is impossible to make these decisions.

## Questions that you or your relative may want to ask about the illness

Below are some of the questions that people often want to discuss with the doctor. You or your relative may also want to ask more specific questions about the illness and treatment. Some questions you may want to ask about treatment are listed on page 17. Many doctors and nurses wait to be asked for information, so don't hesitate to ask and keep on asking.

- Can you be sure that the illness is terminal?
- What are the options?
- What treatment is available and what is the purpose of treatment?
- What can be done to help fight the disease?
- How will the illness develop – what symptoms can your relative expect?
- Will he have a lot of pain?

■ How much time will he have to spend in hospital?
■ Will he need extra help at home if the illness gets worse?
■ How long has he got?

Although there may be no cure for the illness, no one can predict exactly what will happen. But most people want to know what the possibilities are and what the benefits of treatment are likely to be, and at some point during the progress of the illness, they may want to know how long they can expect to live. It is often impossible for a doctor to answer this question – an illness progresses at different rates in different people. But the doctor may be able to answer a more specific question like 'Will the illness affect my plans to go on holiday this summer?'

## Who to ask

The doctor who is caring for your relative is the best person to answer questions about the illness and treatment, as he or she will know all the details of the case.

■ Your friend or relative's **GP (general practitioner)** can answer questions about caring for him at home.
■ The GP may refer your relative to a specialist or **consultant**, usually based at a hospital. If the illness is complicated, the consultant may also involve other specialist doctors. The consultant should write to the GP about the diagnosis, tests and treatment.

These are some of the specialists you may come across:

**Cardiologist** Specialises in heart disease.

**Geriatrician** Specialises in treating older people.

**Haematologist** Specialises in blood disorders such as leukaemia.

**Oncologist** Cancer specialist.

**Psychogeriatrician** Specialises in mental illnesses in older people, including confusion and dementia.

**Specialist in palliative care** Specialises in the relief of symptoms in terminal illness.

**Urologist** Specialises in disorders of the bladder and urinary tract, including prostate problems.

11

> **Stuart**
>
> 'My wife was mainly under the care of the oncologist, but she also saw at different times a cardiologist and a psychogeriatrician. She didn't know who they all were – just more doctors who asked the same questions all over again.'

Nurses plan and provide nursing care and support for people. These are some of the nurses who may be able to give you information:

**Ward sister, charge nurse or ward manager** The person in charge of a hospital ward.

**Named nurse** In some hospitals one nurse has overall responsibility for the patient and will know most about the patient's nursing care.

**District or community nurse** Provides nursing care, support and advice for people who are being cared for at home.

Some nurses provide specialist care for people with specific illnesses. Some specialist nurses work only at the hospital, some visit at home, and some do both. Ask your relative's GP or the person in charge of the ward whether there is a specialist nurse who could help your relative.

**Mastectomy or breast care nurse** Specialises in caring for women who need surgery for breast cancer.

**Oncology nurse** Specialises in caring for people with cancer.

**Macmillan nurse** Specialises in providing support and advice for people with cancer and other terminal illnesses and their families.

**Palliative care nurse** Specialises in caring for people with a terminal illness.

**Stoma nurse** Specialises in caring for people who have had a colostomy.

# Getting more information

People facing a terminal illness and those who are caring for them often feel that they don't get enough information from doctors and nurses. This can happen for all sorts of reasons. If you are worried about this, remember that it is almost always possible to find ways of getting the information you need.

## Why are you not getting enough information?

It may be helpful to look at why you don't seem to be getting enough information. Working out the reasons may help you to decide what to do about it.

- Sometimes patients and carers are given quite a lot of information but are too shocked and upset to absorb what they have been told.
- The doctor may at first give only general or partial information because he or she realises that people who are told they have a terminal illness usually need time before they are ready to know more.
- Sometimes a doctor is deliberately evasive because he or she finds it difficult and distressing to have to talk to someone about dying.
- Occasionally the doctor may believe it is not in the patient's interest to know the whole truth.
- The doctor may be unable to give clearer information because it is not possible to predict how the illness will develop. Living with this uncertainty is distressing for both patients and carers, but it is often an inevitable part of living with the illness.

## Where to go for more information

If you want more information about medical care or treatment in hospital, ask to see the consultant. If necessary, phone the consultant's secretary and ask for an appointment. Ask the ward sister or ward manager for advice if you find the consultant difficult to approach. They may suggest another senior doctor in the consultant's team who is more sympathetic.

If you want more information about nursing care in hospital, or about what care will be needed after discharge from hospital, you could talk to the ill person's named nurse, or the ward sister, charge nurse or ward manager. They should also be able to tell you if there is a nurse who specialises in your relative's condition.

If you want more information about medical care or treatment at home, or services available through the local hospice, make an appointment to talk to your relative's GP. The GP may also be able to help if you cannot get the information you need from hospital staff.

**Note** If your relative's first language is not English, there may be a hospital or community interpreter or patient advocate who can interpret for him and ask questions on his behalf. Ask the ward sister or GP's receptionist, or contact the local Council for Racial Equality or Community Health Council (Health Council in Scotland).

# For more *i*nformation

*i* A helpline or national voluntary organisation concerned with the illness – see the list of organisations on pages 95–108. Organisations may also offer information booklets; a network of local branches or support groups for people with the illness or their carers, or contact people who can give information and advice; a regular newsletter.

*i* A local self-help or support group for people with the illness or for carers – ask your local Community Health Council (Health Council in Scotland) or the Self-help Centre (address on p 106), which has a database of local and national groups for specific illnesses and disabilities.

*i* Other patients and carers – the consultant, GP or district nurse may be able to put you in touch with other people with the illness or other carers.

## Talking with professionals

Some doctors and nurses are very approachable and sympathetic, but others can be intimidating. Sometimes patients and carers are given different information and advice by different doctors. Sometimes dealing with professionals is frustrating and even distressing. There are no simple solutions to this problem, but some of the suggestions below may be useful. They apply to any situation where you need to discuss things with a professional – not just to talking with doctors and nurses.

**Be clear about what you want** This may seem obvious, but have you worked out in your own mind whether you need information about the illness, treatment or prognosis (the expected course of the disease); information about other services or sources of support; or someone to talk to about how you or your relative is feeling?

**Make a list of the questions that you want to ask** If you have prepared a list of points to discuss there is less chance that you will forget something important. Keep the list somewhere handy so that you can add more questions as you think of them.

**Let the person know how soon and for how long you need to talk to them** It is helpful if you can give a doctor, nurse or secretary some idea of how urgent or important the conversation is, and how much time you need. A 15 or 20 minute appointment can often be arranged much sooner than a longer one.

**Consider whether a phone call would do instead of an appointment** Most of us expect to go and see professionals such as doctors in person, often by appointment, but it may be quicker and easier to talk to a doctor or nurse on the phone. If it is appropriate, most health professionals are happy to talk over the phone.

**Be prepared to see the other person's point of view** Accept that doctors and nurses are only human and that communication is not always as good as it should be. Some doctors and nurses wait for patients and families to ask them questions rather than rushing into details that they are not ready to hear. Sometimes a doctor or nurse is unable to answer questions with any certainty.

**Be persistent** Sometimes things go wrong. If the expected test results haven't arrived at the surgery, or the appointment you are waiting for doesn't come in the post, phone again. If you ask a question and you are not satisfied with the answer, keep on asking. If you feel you are getting nowhere with a particular person, work out if there is anyone else you could talk to.

15

# Making decisions

After learning the diagnosis, your relative may be faced with a number of important decisions. If he still feels fairly well, he will probably want to make most of these decisions himself. But this is a time when many people feel very vulnerable, so he may turn to you or to other relatives or friends for advice, or perhaps ask you to make some decisions for him.

## How you can help

- Don't rush into an important decision – if possible make time to think it over.
- Even if your relative asks you to make a decision for him, try to talk it through with him and find out what he really thinks, so that you make the decision together.
- Make sure you have got enough information. The decisions facing someone with a terminal illness are bound to be difficult and painful, but sometimes they are made more difficult by a lack of information. Don't be reluctant to keep on asking.

### Deciding about treatment

**Marie**

'The doctor explained that my mother had a one in five chance of surviving the treatment, or a maximum of 12 weeks to live without it. Mum and I just held on to each other and cried.'

For someone who has cancer, the most immediate decisions are often about treatment. Your relative may be told it is necessary to undergo surgery or a course of radiotherapy or chemotherapy as soon as possible. He may be offered a choice between different types of treatment. Many people feel they need time to think over a decision about major treatment, which may itself carry a high level of risk or result in serious side-effects.

Decisions are easier to make if you and your relative are well informed about what the treatment involves, but you may need to persist in asking questions in order to get this information. The questions below are largely adapted from *Facing the Challenge of Advanced Cancer* published by BACUP, but they are just as relevant to treatment for other illnesses.

# Questions you or your relative may want to ask about treatment

- What is the suggested treatment?
- What is the aim of the treatment? Is it intended to cure the illness, help your relative to live longer, or deal with his symptoms?
- What benefits can be expected from the treatment?
- What side-effects can be expected?
- Will your relative need to stay in hospital for treatment? If so, for how long?
- If treatments are on an outpatient basis, how long will each one take and how many will be needed?
- Are there alternatives to the suggested treatment?
- What would you (the doctor) do if you were in the ill person's position?

It isn't always necessary to rush into a decision on the spot. In a few cases immediate treatment is necessary, but generally another day or a weekend to think things over won't make much difference. If your relative feels that a little time to take stock would make a big difference, ask your GP or consultant if this is feasible.

## Deciding whether to get a second opinion

### Sabeera

'We discussed whether we should try and get a second opinion. I found out from the GP that the only other specialist in our area was at a hospital 20 miles away. It would have meant a very tiring journey by bus and train so in the end we decided it wasn't worth it.'

If you or your relative is concerned about the diagnosis or treatment, you may want to consider getting a second opinion. But it is helpful to be clear in your own mind why you want to do this. Sometimes there are real concerns about the accuracy of the diagnosis or the benefits of treatment. Sometimes patients or carers want a second or even third opinion because they are still unable to accept that the illness is real – they are still in the 'denial' phase described on page 3. A second opinion which confirms the diagnosis may help the ill person to begin to accept the illness.

The quickest way to get a second opinion is to ask the consultant. But people do not have a right to have a second opinion – some consultants are sympathetic to such a request but others may refuse. Alternatively your relative can go back and ask his GP to refer him to another consultant, but this may take longer.

## Deciding whether to change doctor

If for any reason your relative is unhappy with his consultant or GP he may want to consider changing doctor. It is often helpful to talk this over with someone else first. Sometimes there are very good grounds for changing doctor. But when people are faced with a terminal illness, feelings of anger are very common (see pp 3–4). Sometimes patients and carers direct their anger at the person who bears the bad news – usually the consultant or the GP.

### *How to go about it*

*Changing consultant*

If your relative is not happy with the consultant, you or your relative should explain his concerns to the GP and ask if he can be referred to a different one. It may help if you can give the name of a preferred consultant – get advice about this (see below).

If your relative is to be discharged from hospital, he can ask to be referred to a hospice doctor if the hospice has a home care service. Hospice home care is not just for people in the final stages of illness – see pages 32–33 for more information.

*Changing GP*

To change GP, find a doctor that your relative would like to move to and phone the surgery to see if the doctor is accepting new patients. Most doctors like to see a new patient in person before accepting them. If the doctor is willing to accept your relative, the receptionist will tell you how to register. If you have any difficulty in finding another GP, contact the Health Authority/Health Board in Scotland (look in your local telephone directory). They are responsible for providing GP care and can help you to find a doctor.

# Getting independent advice

- If you have a good relationship with your own or your relative's GP, make an appointment to talk over the problem.

- Contact your local Community Health Council (CHC – called a Health Council in Scotland) to find out the names of other consultants or GPs in your area and ask the CHC secretary for advice.

- Find out if there is a local self-help or support group for people with your relative's illness. The local contact person may know a lot about the consultants who deal with the illness and may be able to reassure you or to suggest the name of a more sympathetic specialist.

- If you can't get more information locally, there may be a national helpline that offers advice to patients and families. Talking things over with a telephone counsellor may help you and your relative to work out the best course of action.

## Deciding who will care

As the illness progresses your relative will probably begin to need help with personal and nursing care. The information in the next chapter will help you and your relative to work out what care is needed, to find out what help is available if he wants to be cared for at home, and what the options are if it becomes impossible to care for him at home any longer. See pages 34–37 for more details about support for carers.

# 3 Getting help with caring

*It is often not possible to predict how a terminal illness will develop or at what point treatment or nursing care will be needed, but the care that your relative needs will change as the illness progresses, so the plans you make in the early stages must be flexible.*

*Most people want to be cared for at home, but the decision may depend on your relative's condition and circumstances and on what support services are available locally. This chapter looks at what support you may be able to get to help you care at home and at alternative forms of care.*

*Caring at home for someone with an advanced illness is difficult and demanding. If you become the main carer you will need to look after yourself and your own health as well as looking after your relative. The last part of the chapter looks at your needs as a carer.*

### Sam

'Sometimes you just feel desperate. It helps to know that other people feel like that too.'

'I was looking after my wife for about a year before she died. Most of that time she was reasonably well – she could get about and go out, although she was weak and got tired very easily. Cooking was the hardest part when she got too ill to do things any more. I got better at it, but I used to buy supermarket ready-cooked meals quite a lot. My daughter came and cooked once a week and left stuff in the fridge, but she lives quite a way away and she's got a young family, so it was difficult for her to get over here more often. When we got Attendance Allowance I decided to pay someone to come and help with the housework. We asked about a home help, but I was told the council doesn't have them any more, and that we probably wouldn't qualify for any help because I'm here.

'I wanted to look after her but I didn't know if I'd be able to manage right to the end. Early on she had a bad bout with an infection and she was incontinent for a while. That was very difficult for both of us. I did feel worried then about whether I'd be able to cope at the end. The district nurse came when she was incontinent and told me we could go and look round the hospice if we thought it might be a good idea for later. If I'm honest, I have to say that I thought it was a good idea. Nancy didn't, but I think she changed her mind when she went there. She started going to the day centre, and she liked the nurses a lot, although she wasn't so keen on some of the patients. She died in the hospice and two of the nurses came to the funeral – I was very touched by that.

'I met the secretary of the carers' group at the hospice open day, and I started going to the group. It was mostly women, but there were three men including me who used to go now and then. It helped, because sometimes you just feel desperate. It helps to know that other people feel like that too.

'I found out about Attendance Allowance through the carers' group, and I found out from the hospice about Crossroads Care attendants and chiropodists who do home visits.

'It's frustrating because you assume that the doctor will tell you what you can get, but they don't. It took me a while to learn that you just have to ask and keep on asking. The hospice social worker was a turning point for us – she knew the system inside out and backwards. Everyone needs someone like her.'

# Deciding whether to care at home

The period in which your relative will need care may be weeks, months or perhaps even years. The care needed will depend on the nature of the illness, the type of treatment offered, and how your relative responds to treatment. Be prepared for the unpredictable, and accept that you may have to change your plans and rethink future arrangements as you go along. For most people thinking about caring or arranging for someone to be cared for at home, there are several key questions:

■   Is it practical for the ill person to continue living at home?
■   What level of care will she need now and in the future?
■   If caring means giving up work, is this the right decision?
■   What are the alternatives to being cared for at home?

What you decide will depend to some extent on your relative's circumstances:

**If she lives alone** she may be able to continue to do so with enough help and support, but she may well need hospital, nursing home or hospice care later on.

**If she lives with you** or someone else who can provide personal and nursing care, it may be possible to provide most of the care at home. You may feel that you want to do this for as long as possible, but later on you or your relative may decide that hospital, nursing home or hospice care would be better.

**If she comes to live with you or you move in with her**, you will need to have a realistic idea of how much care she will need and for how long. You will have to think about whether this arrangement will be practical in the long term, especially if there are other members of the family to consider.

Your decision may also depend on what alternative forms of care are available locally. This may vary widely, depending where you live.

# Alternative forms of care

| **Regular or short-term care** | **Provided by** |
| --- | --- |
| Sitter or care attendant – someone to look after your relative for a few hours | *Social services, voluntary organisation, private organisation – contact United Kingdom Home Care Association (UKHCA)* |
| 'Twilight' or 'tucking in' service – someone to help her get up or go to bed | |
| Live-in help if she needs constant care | *Private organisation – contact UKHCA or advertise and employ someone yourself directly* |
| Day centre, day hospital, day care away from home | *Social services, voluntary organisation, hospice, Health Authority/Health Board* |
| Residential home, nursing home, hospital or hospice for a residential stay for your relative, from a few days to a few weeks | *Social services, Health Authority/Health Board, voluntary organisation, private organisation. Contact one of the national associations for care homes (see below). For a hospice contact the Hospice Information Service* |
| Holiday in special holiday centre or adapted accommodation, sometimes with companions or care attendants | *Social services or private specialist company – contact Holiday Care Service or RADAR* |

| **Longer-term care** | **Provided by** |
| --- | --- |
| Residential home – for someone who needs help with daily living, but not nursing care | *Social services, voluntary organisation, private organisation – contact National Care Homes Association* |

| | |
|---|---|
| Nursing home – for someone who needs nursing care provided by qualified nurses | *Usually private individual or company – contact Registered Nursing Home Association or Health Authority Registration Unit* |
| Hospice – for someone with a terminal illness, staffed by health and social services professionals | *Voluntary organisation – contact Hospice Information Service* |

## What care does your relative need?

Here are some of the questions to which you and your relative might want answers if you are thinking of caring for her at home.

- How mobile will she be?
- Will she be able to wash and dress herself and get to the toilet without help?
- Will she need any special aids or equipment, or adaptations to the home?
- Will she be safe at home on her own, or will she need someone there all the time?
- What medicines will she need to take? What are they for? How should they be taken and when?
- Will she need a special diet? Are there foods that she should or shouldn't have? Does she need any dietary supplements?
- Will she need to attend an outpatient clinic or go into hospital for further tests or treatments? How often?
- Can she get help with transport to hospital?

Note You and your relative will also need to think about how the illness and caring at home will affect your finances, for example if you have to give up work. See pages 39–46 for more information, especially the questions on page 40.

## Who to ask

Although no one can be certain about how your relative's illness will progress, it will help your planning if you are well informed at an early stage about how the illness is likely to develop and the options for caring. The hospital doctor, the GP or one of the nurses described on page 12 will be able to answer some questions about care at home. The chart on pages 27–30 lists other professionals or organisations who can help in planning or arranging home care.

# What help is available at home?

In most areas there is a range of support and practical help available for someone with a terminal illness who is being cared for at home. The services available and the way they are organised vary widely from area to area.

If your relative is discharged from hospital, hospital staff should arrange for any immediate care or treatment that she will need on coming home. Ask the nurse in charge of the ward or the hospital social worker what help the hospital can arrange.

## Getting an assessment

You can also ask social services for an **assessment** of your relative's needs if you think she needs extra help at home with personal care, or services such as meals on wheels or a home help, or perhaps help with adaptations or repairs to enable her to move about, wash properly or keep warm in cold weather. Phone your local social services office and explain the situation to the **duty officer**, who will put you in touch with the person who deals with assessments.

Since April 1993, councils have a duty to assess the needs of anyone who appears to need community care services. They also have a duty to assess people with disabilities. The waiting time for an assessment depends on how much help the ill person needs, and varies from area to area. If there is a deterioration in your relative's condition or circumstances which makes her more vulnerable, let social services know, as she may become a higher priority for assessment. If you are providing a substantial amount of care to your relative on a regular basis, you also have the right to ask the local authority to consider your needs as a carer when they are assessing your relative's needs.

Once your relative's needs have been assessed, the social services department will decide whether they can offer help. If they do decide to help, a **key worker** or **care manager** should be allocated to arrange services for the person needing care and the carer. If your relative is found to also have health or housing needs, social services should notify the relevant authorities.

Many carers find that the help and support on offer is much more limited than they expected. If you feel like this, don't be afraid to ask for more help. An important part of your role as a carer will be to find out what services are available and whether you are eligible for them. Be prepared to ask for information and keep on asking. Because services are limited and the number of people needing help with caring is growing, the professionals you come in contact with may not volunteer information about services unless you ask specifically.

Note Since March 1997, local authorities can take their own resources into account when deciding whether someone has a need for a service under the Chronically Sick and Disabled Persons Act 1970, and which services they will then arrange or provide. Services cannot be withdrawn or reduced until the person's care needs have been assessed (or reassessed) against revised eligibility criteria. Any reduction in, withdrawal of, or refusal to provide services must not leave individuals at severe physical risk.

The chart below provides brief information about the people and services that may be available in your area to help with caring at home. There is more information about some of these key professionals and services at the end of the chart.

# Medical, nursing and other care at home

| Organisation/ person | What is offered | How to contact |
|---|---|---|
| General practitioner (GP) | *24-hour medical care at home for people registered with them* | *At GP's surgery* |
| Macmillan nurse | *Emotional support and expert advice on advanced cancer and other terminal illness, especially control of symptoms* | *Ask the GP or hospital doctor, or contact Cancer Relief Macmillan Fund or Cancerlink for details of your nearest Macmillan nurse team* |
| District or community nurse or private nurse | *Nursing care at home. Some areas have 'twilight' and night nursing services. Advice on lifting* | *Contact district nurse direct (phone number listed under the Health Authority/Health Board) or ask the GP. Contact private nursing agency* |
| Marie Curie nurse | *Nurse trained in cancer care to stay with sick person for periods up to 24 hours* | *Through district nurse or Macmillan nurse* |
| Care attendant/ personal care assistant/ personal care aide | *Help with daily personal care for sick person. Not skilled nursing, eg they don't do dressings or injections* | *Through social services, voluntary organisation (contact United Kingdom Home Care Association)* |
| Physiotherapist | *Treatment and exercises to help mobility. Advice on lifting* | *Through the GP or hospital physiotherapy department* |
| Specialist nurse adviser | *Specialist advice for particular problems, eg stoma care, incontinence* | *Ask the GP or district nurse or phone the Incontinence Information Helpline on 0191–213 0050* |

# Practical help at home

| Organisation/ person | What is offered | How to contact |
|---|---|---|
| Home help/ home care worker/home care assistant | Help with housework and shopping. Varies in different areas; some now also offer personal care | Through home help organiser at social services, voluntary organisation or private agency |
| Meals on wheels | Hot midday meal brought to your home | Through social services or voluntary organisation (GP may arrange this) |
| Local volunteer groups | Help may include gardening, DIY jobs in the house, lifts for outings or hospital visits | Citizens Advice Bureaux, local Councils for Voluntary Service and public libraries have information on local volunteer groups |
| Laundry service | May be available if incontinence is a problem | Through social services in some areas (arranged through district nurse) or private laundry service |

# Aids and equipment

| Organisation/ person | What is offered | How to contact |
|---|---|---|
| British Red Cross | Short-term loans of equipment such as folding wheelchairs and commodes | Phone number of local branch under British Red Cross |
| District or Macmillan nurse | Short-term loans of nursing equipment such as sheepskins and special mattresses to help prevent pressure sores | Contact district nurse or Macmillan nurse as described above |

| | | |
|---|---|---|
| Occupational therapist | *Advice on aids and adaptations in the home to help sick person retain independence* | *Through social services or hospital* |
| Disabled Living Foundation | *Advice on aids and equipment and where to buy them* | *Address on page 100* |

# Organisations that can make special financial grants

| **Organisation/ person** | *What is offered* | *How to contact* |
|---|---|---|
| Cancer Relief Macmillan Fund | *Grants for essential items for people with cancer, eg help with heating costs or installation of telephone* | *Through social services, Macmillan nurse, district nurse or GP* |
| Marie Curie Cancer Care | *Grants for items needed for home nursing for someone with cancer, eg bed clothes* | *Through district nurse or Macmillan nurse* |
| Counsel and Care | *Grants for elderly people needing care at home* | *Through social services* |

# Information and support

| **Organisation/ person** | *What is offered* | *How to contact* |
|---|---|---|
| Citizens Advice Bureau (CAB) | *Independent, confidential advice on legal and financial matters and other sources of help* | *Look in your local telephone directory* |

| | | |
|---|---|---|
| Community Health Council | *Information on local health services and advice if something goes wrong* | *Look in your local telephone directory* |
| Carers National Association | *Information and support for carers, including young carers. Local carers' self-help groups* | *Address on page 98* |
| Age Concern | *Information, support and practical help for older people. Local groups, clubs and day centres* | *See page 109* |
| Counsel and Care | *Information and support for older people* | *Address on page 100* |
| Local churches and other religious groups | *Spiritual and emotional support. Many also offer practical support* | *Details on notice boards of religious groups' buildings or in local libraries* |
| Hospice Information Service | *Information on hospices and specialist home care throughout the UK* | *Address on page 102* |
| Social worker | *Help in organising services at home, applying for benefits and grants. Counselling support* | *At local social services department, hospice or hospital social work department* |

# Key people or organisations providing medical care at home

## General practitioner (GP)

If your relative is being cared for at home, the GP is one of the key people who can refer her to other professionals or put you in contact with other services. If your relative is coming home from hospital, the consultant should write to the GP with details of the diagnosis and treatment.

If you are worried about symptoms, or any aspect of your relative's care or treatment at home, don't feel reluctant to contact the doctor. Sometimes communication between hospital doctors and GPs is not as efficient as it should be. Sometimes the GP is not aware of the situation or assumes, unless he or she hears otherwise, that the person who is ill and those caring for her are coping.

As the illness progresses, your relative may develop more symptoms or other health problems. Although it may not be possible to cure the illness, most symptoms can be controlled or relieved. Always tell the GP about persistent symptoms or problems. See pages 55–60 for more information about symptoms.

### District nurse or community nurse

District nurses (now sometimes known as community nurses) work with GPs and other professionals. They can give practical nursing help and advice on caring for someone who is ill at home. A district nurse may be able to teach you how to carry out nursing tasks such as lifting, changing a dressing or giving an injection. They can give you advice about equipment, aids or other services to help with caring.

In some areas the district nursing service also provides twilight nurses for people who need help with getting up and going to bed, or night nurses for those who need constant care through the night.

### Marie Curie nurse

Marie Curie nurses are specially trained to provide day or night nursing care for people with cancer being cared for at home. In addition to providing specialised nursing care, they can also provide nursing help to give other family members a break or the opportunity of a good night's sleep.

### Macmillan nurse

Macmillan nurses are specially trained to provide care and support for people who have been diagnosed as having an illness that cannot be cured. They do not generally do practical nursing tasks like

31

bathing or changing dressings, but they work closely with GPs and can help with pain relief and symptom control. They are trained in counselling and can provide valuable emotional support for the person who is ill, the carer and other family members.

## Hospice services

Most people think of a hospice as providing inpatient care for someone in the last stages of a terminal illness. Today most hospices also provide some form of care and support for people with a terminal illness living at home and their families. The person needing care does not have to be very ill or weak to use these services. Hospices aim to help people with a terminal illness to achieve the best possible quality of life from the point of diagnosis until they die, wherever they are being cared for.

Most hospices have doctors who specialise in the control of pain and other distressing symptoms, and are available to give advice to GPS, hospital doctors, and specialist and community nurses. A few hospices work within the NHS but most are independent charitable foundations, so the services that they provide tend to vary. Your local hospice may offer some of these services for people being cared for at home:

**Respite care** A short-term residential stay for the person who is ill in order to control symptoms or give the carer a break.

**An outpatient clinic.**

**A home care team** which provides care and support at home for the ill person and their family.

**A volunteer service** Some hospices can arrange volunteer sitters, or a volunteer to drive the ill person to day care or clinic appointments.

**Day care** Activities, usually lunch, and a chance to talk to other people who understand what it is like to have a terminal illness.

To find out about your local hospice, ask your GP or look at the *Directory of Hospice Services*, available from the Hospice Information Service (address on p 102). Hospice care is free, and there is not usually a waiting list. Many people are apprehensive about what a hospice will be like, but hospice staff are usually happy to show you round if you would like to visit.

## Pain relief clinics

Some hospitals have pain relief clinics run by a consultant, usually an anaesthetist, who specialises in the control and relief of pain. The GP or hospital consultant may refer your relative to the clinic if they feel this would be appropriate.

## Hospital support team, continuing care or palliative care unit

Some hospitals have a specialised team which provides care and support for inpatients or outpatients with a terminal illness. The team usually includes nurses, who are trained in counselling and symptom control, and sometimes a doctor, social worker and chaplain. Some hospitals also have a special inpatients unit, called a continuing care or palliative care unit, which is run in much the same way as a hospice.

Note  Since April 1996, health authorities have had to publish and operate policies, plans and eligibility criteria for a range of NHS continuing health care services, including palliative care. Further details are contained in Age Concern England Factsheet 37 *Hospital discharge arrangements and NHS continuing health care services.*

## Home care team

This is a specialised team, similar to a hospital support team, which works in the community with ill people who are being cared for at home. Home care teams are usually based at a hospital or hospice and sometimes include a doctor who shares the patient's care with the GP.

# Checklist: practical preparations for caring at home

If you are caring for someone who is coming home from hospital, there may be some practical preparations you can make to help with caring.

**Instructions about medicines and diet** If your relative needs to take several medicines or follow a special diet, ask the hospital nurses or dietician to help you draw up a chart or write down the instructions.

**Lifting safely** If your relative is too weak to stand or change position in bed, you will need to move or lift her. Ask a nurse or physiotherapist to teach you how to do this safely so that you don't risk injuring yourself.

**The bedroom** If your relative cannot get up or down stairs easily, think about moving her bedroom downstairs if this is possible. It might be worth rearranging the furniture, perhaps so that she can get in and out of bed more easily, or see out of the window from an armchair.

**Getting to the toilet** If there is no downstairs toilet, a commode could be useful – the district nurse can give advice about borrowing one.

**Aids and equipment** Things like grab rails, a seat in the shower or bath or a raised toilet seat can make the difference between your relative being able to do things for herself and depending on other people for help. An occupational therapist can give advice about aids, equipment and other adaptations that can help her remain independent for as long as possible.

# Your needs as a carer

So far we have looked at the needs of the ill person and at what support may be available to help with the practical side of caring. But carers also need support with the emotional side of caring.

As we have seen, carers often go through the same reactions to the illness as the sick person (see pp 2–5). Feelings of loss and grief are very common in the early stages. As well as feeling grief at the approaching death of the person you love, you may also feel regret for the 'normal' life you may be losing, for the job you may have to give up in order to care, at being cut off from normal contact with friends, relatives or workmates.

Feelings of anger and resentment are also common. The carer's world is turned upside down, and these are natural reactions. Sometimes the carer's feelings of anger and resentment are turned on the ill person. This may happen only occasionally or it may happen a lot. If you find you are feeling increasingly angry and resentful it is important to try and do something about it. Sometimes just finding someone to talk to can help to get things back in perspective. Sometimes getting extra help with caring or getting a regular break can make the difference between being overwhelmed by your feelings and staying on top of them.

## Your relationship with the person you care for

Illness tends to bring out the worst as well as the best in a relationship. A terminal illness can bring people closer together, but it can also make any strain or tension between them worse. Sometimes it does both at the same time. The ill person and those close to her may hope that the crisis will bring about a positive change in their relationships, but this doesn't often happen. People tend to die as they have lived. Someone who has been difficult all her life is not likely to stop being difficult because she is ill.

Even when you have a close relationship with the person needing care, caring drains your energy and resilience. It can also be distressing if the person you care for becomes very confused or physically altered by the illness. You may feel she is no longer the person you used to love.

## Looking after yourself

Carers have needs of their own which are separate to and different from the needs of the person they care for. Recognising your own needs and doing something about them isn't selfish – caring is tiring and stressful and carers who don't look after themselves and recharge their batteries now and then sometimes become ill themselves. Spend a little time thinking about how you can increase the support you are getting for yourself. Do you need:

- a few hours off from caring on a regular basis;
- respite care (from a few days to a couple of weeks);
- regular company for your relative apart from you;
- someone your relative can talk to about how she's feeling;
- someone to talk to about how you're feeling;
- a social activity to take your mind off caring for a few hours each week.

There may be a local support group or self-help group for carers. Not everyone likes the idea of a carers group, but it can help to talk to other people who understand exactly what you're going through. The GP, Macmillan nurse or district nurse may be able to put you in touch with a carers' group, or with other individual carers if you feel that a group is not for you.

# For more _i_nformation

_i_ _You and Caring: An action plan for caring at home_ by Penny Mares, a self-help book designed to help carers solve problems and feel more in control, published by the King's Fund Centre. Available from Grantham Books Services, Isaac Newton Way, Alma Park Industrial Estate, Grantham, Lincs NG31 9SD. Tel: 01476 541 080.

_i_ _The Support You Need: Information for carers of Afro-Caribbean elderly people_ by Linda Eribo, published by the King's Fund Centre. Available from Grantham Books Services (address above).

_i_ _Dekhbaal lai pukkar/Call for Care: For Asian carers of elderly people_ by Yasmin Guneratuam, published by the King's Fund Centre/Health Education Authority. Available in Bengali, English, Gujarati, Punjabi and Urdu from Grantham Books Services (address above).

_i_ _Where to Go From Here? A handbook for Chinese carers_ by Wing and Kerrie Au, published by the Health Education Authority. Available from the HEA, Distribution Department, Hamilton House, Mabledon Place, London WC1H 9TX.

_i_ _Who Cares Now? Caring for an older person_ by Nancy Kohner and Penny Mares, published by BBC Education. Provides general information about the practical and emotional aspects of caring for an older person. Available from Who Cares Now?, PO Box 7, London W3 6XJ.

*ℹ* *Caring at Home When Cancer Cannot be Cured*, published by CancerLink (address on p 98).

*ℹ* *Coping at Home: Caring for someone with advanced cancer*, published by BACUP (address on p 96).

*ℹ* **The Carers National Association** (address on p 98) provides information, advice and support to carers of all ages. Their **Young Carers Project** is especially for young people who are caring.

37

# 4 Money and legal matters

*Being ill or caring for someone usually involves extra expense. It may mean larger heating bills or buying a new bed; it may involve giving up work or paying someone to help with caring. The first part of this chapter provides information about benefits and other financial help for people with a terminal illness and for carers.*

*The ill person may also want to think about legal arrangements that will make it easier for someone to take over his affairs in the later stages of the illness and to sort things out after his death. If your relative hasn't made a Will, it is a good idea to consider making one now. The second part of the chapter provides information about taking over responsibility for someone's affairs, making a Will, making a 'living will' and other practical arrangements.*

## Isobel

'I was really glad that there was a bit of money saved because it was the only thing that kept me going.'

'I phoned the district nurse to ask advice about something else, and she said, "Do you know about applying for Attendance Allowance?" I didn't, but she said I should ask the GP about it. The doctor said, "I think you're right, it probably is time to apply." I was horrified to see the bit on the application form about the person not being expected to live longer than six months. He said, "Well, no one can say with certainty how long your sister will live, and even if you don't need to pay for care now, there may come a time when you do have to. In any case, the money will certainly come in useful for something.

'Although the doctor wrote on the form that Marion was likely to die within six months, in fact she lived another 14 months. Towards the end I asked social services about getting a sitter or a nurse at night. A friend of mine, who lives some way away, had suggested this might be possible, but they said their local practice was to provide someone only if the carer was actually ill in bed. We had a neighbour who works part-time in a nursing home, and for the last three months I paid her to come in for a couple of nights a week to sit with Marion so I could get some sleep. I was really glad that there was a bit of money saved to be able to do that, because it was the only thing that kept me going.'

# The costs of caring

As carer your first concern will be the care and comfort of the person who needs looking after, but it is worth thinking about your short-term and longer-term financial needs from the start. The questions below are designed to help you do this. The list may look daunting, but it covers a wide range of different circumstances. Only some of the questions will be relevant to you.

**Note** **Your relative may be eligible for some help free or at a low cost – see the chart on pages 27–30. How much help is available may depend on your relative's income and on how services are organised in your area. In some areas services are patchy, and some may be available only if you are able to pay.**

## What costs do you need to think about?

Will your relative need to consider:

- giving up work or changing to part-time work;
- moving to more suitable accommodation;
- moving the bedroom downstairs, if he finds it difficult to get up and down stairs;
- buying new furniture – for example, a bed or armchair – to make him more comfortable;
- extra heating to keep him warm;
- a telephone to enable him to get in touch with a doctor quickly, or to keep in touch with friends and relatives;
- ways of getting around outside the home – for example, using taxis or extra running costs for a car or adapting an existing car for wheelchair access;
- someone to help with jobs around the house, or with personal or nursing care?

If you are the main carer, will you also need to consider:

- giving up work or changing to part-time work to care for your relative (if the answer is yes, how will this affect your pension?);
- paying someone to help with caring so that you can go out or get a good night's sleep now and then (if your relative is not eligible for free help)?

**Note** **If you are thinking about big changes such as moving house or making major adaptations to the home, it is worth talking these over first with the hospital doctor or GP. If it would make a big difference to your relative's quality of life it may be well worth the expense. If your relative has only weeks or months to live, he may find that a major change is more upsetting than it is worth.**

# What help is available?

There are special benefits to help people who are very ill or disabled and those who care for them. If you or your relative has a low income, you may also be able to get Income Support, Housing

Benefit or Council Tax Benefit. If either of you already gets benefits, the amount you are entitled to may change because of the illness. The benefit system is complicated, so it is worth getting advice about what you can claim.

**Note** Welfare advice centres such as the Citizens Advice Bureau know their way round the benefit system and can save you a lot of time.

# Benefits for people who are very ill or disabled

## *Attendance Allowance*

This is a tax-free weekly cash benefit for people who need help with personal care, supervision, or to have someone watching over them and who become ill or disabled at or after age 65 or who become disabled at a younger age but only make a claim after they reach 65. It is paid at two levels: you get the higher level if you need help during the day and the night; you get the lower level if you need help either during the day or during the night. It does not depend on National Insurance (NI) benefits and is not affected by savings or income. It may be paid on top of other benefits.

To get Attendance Allowance the person who is ill should normally have needed help with personal care for six months, even if no one is actually giving care at the time they apply. Under special rules, people with a terminal illness who may not live longer than six months can get the allowance straight away – they do not have to wait until they have needed help for six months.

**Note** An application for Attendance Allowance or the care component of DLA (see below) can be made by another person on behalf of someone who is terminally ill, so it is possible for someone to receive an allowance under the special rules without knowing their diagnosis.

## *Disability Living Allowance (DLA)*

This has replaced Attendance Allowance for people who become sick or disabled before the age of 65 and claim before their 65th birthday. It has a care component for people who need help with personal care, supervision or watching over, paid at three different levels, and a mobility component for people who have difficulty in getting around, paid at two different levels. It is not taxable, is not affected by NI contributions, income or savings, and may be paid on top of other benefits.

To get DLA the person who is ill should normally have needed help for at least three months and be likely to need it for at least a further six months. Under special rules, people with a terminal illness who may not live longer than six months can get the allowance straight away.

Although you need to claim DLA before your 65th birthday, once it is being paid it can continue after that age.

**Note** **People whose homes have certain features which are important for a disabled person, such as extra space for a wheelchair, may qualify for a reduction in their Council Tax bill under the 'disability reduction scheme'.**

## *Other benefits for people who become sick or disabled while they are working*

There is a range of benefits to help people who become ill while they are working. These include:

**Statutory Sick Pay (SSP)** Paid by the employer for the first 28 weeks to someone who is too sick or disabled to work.

**Incapacity Benefit** For people unable to work due to sickness or disability. It depends on NI contributions and normally stops at pension age.

**Severe Disablement Allowance** For people of working age who cannot claim Incapacity Benefit because they have not paid enough NI contributions.

There are also specific benefits to help people who have become sick or disabled as the result of their work or a war injury.

# For more *i*nformation

ⓘ Age Concern England Factsheet 18 *A brief guide to money benefits.*

ⓘ *Your Rights*, a comprehensive guide to money benefits for older people, published annually by Age Concern Books (details on p 111).

ⓘ DSS leaflet FB 28 *Sick or Disabled?* Includes a full explanation of benefits to help people who become sick or disabled while they are working.

ⓘ DSS leaflet Nl 9 *Going into Hospital?* Explains how going into hospital affects social security benefits and pensions.

## Benefits for carers

### *Invalid Care Allowance (ICA)*

This is a benefit for people of working age (16–64) who cannot work full-time because they are looking after someone. You may be able to get ICA if you spend at least 35 hours a week looking after a person who gets the care component of Disability Living Allowance at the middle or highest rate, Attendance Allowance or Constant Attendance Allowance.

ICA 'overlaps' with other benefits, so if you are already receiving certain State benefits or pensions these may reduce or cancel out the ICA completely. It may still be worth claiming, however: if you are getting Income Support, Housing Benefit or Council Tax Benefit you will receive higher rates of these benefits if you are entitled to ICA (see below).

Note  If the person you care for is getting the severe disability premium paid with Income Support, it could be affected if you claim ICA for yourself. If in doubt, ask the Citizens Advice Bureau what you should do.

### *The carer premium*

This is an extra amount of money paid to someone who is getting Income Support, Housing Benefit or Council Tax Benefit. You will be entitled to the carer premium if you are entitled to Invalid Care Allowance (even if you don't actually receive ICA because you are already getting other benefits).

# For more *i*nformation

ℹ️ DSS leaflet FB 31 *Caring for Someone?* – a guide to benefits for carers and for people with a disability.

ℹ️ The Carers National Association produce a range of leaflets for carers. Their address is on page 98.

## Benefits for people on low incomes

You may be able to get other benefits or help with costs if you or the person you care for is on a low income. These are summarised below. You can get more information about specific benefits from the leaflets listed at the end of this section.

**Income Support** For people aged 60 or over who do not need to 'sign on' as unemployed. To qualify, people must have no more than £8,000 savings (£16,000 for care home residents) and income below a certain amount.

**Housing Benefit** Help with the cost of rent for people on Income Support or a low income and with no more than £16,000 savings.

**Council Tax Benefit** Help with the Council Tax for people on Income Support or a low income and with no more than £16,000 savings.

**The Social Fund** Makes lump-sum payments in the form of a grant or loan to help people on low incomes with exceptional expenses.

**Help with NHS costs** Help with fares to and from hospital, dental treatment, glasses and sight tests, wigs, elastic stockings and fabric supports.

**Prescriptions** Free for men and women aged 60 and over. People who suffer from specific illnesses also get free prescriptions. A prescription season ticket will save money if someone needs more than 5 prescriptions in 4 months or more than 14 prescriptions in 12 months.

# For more *i*nformation

*ⓘ* Age Concern England Factsheet 25 *Income Support and the Social Fund.*

*ⓘ* Age Concern England Factsheet 17 *Housing Benefit and Council Tax Benefit.*

*ⓘ* Age Concern England Factsheet 21 *The Council Tax and older people.*

*ⓘ* **Benefit Enquiry Line** (0800 88 22 00) for free and confidential advice about benefits for people with disabilities and their carers. Advisers can go through a claim form over the phone and fill it in for you or your relative.

*ⓘ* **Citizens Advice Bureau** (look in the phone book) for advice and help in working out what benefits you should claim.

*ⓘ* Ask the **hospital social worker** or **medical social worker** attached to the GP's surgery or health centre, the **Macmillan nurse** or the **district nurse** for advice about benefits and other financial help for people with a terminal illness and their carers.

## Sorting out pension rights

If your relative is diagnosed as terminally ill while he is still in work, he should check what he is entitled to under his occupational pension scheme.

■ If someone has to leave work before retirement age because of illness, they may be entitled to income from their pension scheme.

■ If someone dies while they are still working, most occupational pension schemes provide a death-in-service lump-sum payment and a pension for the spouse or dependent children of the employee.

■ If someone with a terminal illness has no dependents, it is sometimes possible to commute the pension in full – in other words, to exchange the right to a pension in the future for an immediate lump-sum payment. This could help to pay for care, to adapt the home to make it more suitable, to pay for a special holiday or perhaps a final trip to see relatives who live abroad.

Your relative should look over his contract of employment and talk to the personnel officer. A trade union or professional association may also give advice and support if problems arise in dealing with the employer. Some professional associations and trade unions also provide sickness and death benefits for members.

If your relative has any problems with an occupational pension that he cannot sort out with his employer or pension provider, he should contact the Pensions Advisory Service (address on p 105).

Note **If your relative is a member of a personal pension scheme, he should contact the company that runs the scheme to find out what benefits he and his dependents may be entitled to.**

## For more *i*nformation

*i* *The Pensions Handbook*, published by Age Concern Books (details on p 111).

# Taking over responsibility for someone's affairs

As his illness progresses, your relative may want to discuss ways in which you or someone else can help him manage his affairs. At a later stage he may wish to appoint someone to take over the management of his affairs completely.

## If the ill person is mentally capable

### Collecting benefits or pension

Someone who is ill can nominate an agent to collect his State Pension and any other benefits from the post office.

### Access to bank and building society accounts

Someone who is physically unable to get to the bank or building society can authorise another person to use his account. This is known as a **third party mandate**. A third party mandate should not be used if the ill person becomes incapable of understanding what is happening.

## Power of attorney

This gives someone the legal right to manage another person's affairs, for example if he is ill in hospital. An **ordinary power of attorney** remains valid only as long as the person giving it is capable of giving instructions. You can buy a special document to create a power of attorney from a legal stationer, or you can ask a solicitor to draw one up for you.

# If the ill person is mentally incapable

## Receiving benefits for the ill person

If the ill person is not capable of understanding what he is doing, the Department of Social Security can make you his **appointee**. As appointee you can claim and collect social security benefits and pensions on his behalf and spend it on his needs.

## Enduring power of attorney

In England and Wales, an enduring power of attorney remains valid even if the person giving it later becomes mentally incapable. But the person giving it must be mentally capable at the time of signing the document.

'Mentally capable' means that the person fully understands the nature of the power they are giving to the attorney, and that the power cannot be revoked if they should become mentally incapable. Someone who is becoming confused may still be mentally capable for hours or days at a time between bouts of confusion, and fully able to understand the effects of giving someone enduring power of attorney. To avoid the risk of any future dispute, if there is doubt about your relative's ability to understand, you may wish to ask a doctor to be present and to witness your relative's signature.

An enduring power of attorney can appoint you to take over some-one's affairs straight away, or it can come into effect only in certain conditions, for example when the attorney believes that the donor is becoming or has become mentally incapacitated, or if the doctor diagnoses the ill person as mentally incapable. It is a good idea to discuss such conditions with your relative and write them into the document. Sometimes people do this at the same time as making their Will.

### Applying to the Court of Protection

In England and Wales, if the ill person becomes mentally incapable of managing his own affairs and has not given someone else enduring power of attorney, it may be necessary to apply to the Court of Protection for authorisation to manage his money.

The Court will usually appoint and supervise a **receiver** to manage his affairs. However, if he has little assets and his affairs are straightforward, the Public Trust Office (which is responsible for the day-to-day administration of those cases under the jurisdiction of the Court of Protection) may give **directions** or make a **short order** (instead of a receivership order) giving directions as to how the individual's affairs should be organised.

Applying to the Court of Protection is often costly and complicated; it is better to avoid it if you can by encouraging your relative to create an enduring power of attorney in good time.

# For more *i*nformation

*ⓘ* To find out more about the Court of Protection or to make an application, contact them at the address on page 100.

*ⓘ* *Enduring Power of Attorney* and *Handbook for Receivers*, available free from the Public Trust Office. Send a large sae to the address on page 100.

*ⓘ* Age Concern England Factsheet 22 *Legal arrangements for managing financial affairs.*

*ⓘ* *Managing Other People's Money*, published by Age Concern Books (details on p 112).

# Managing someone else's affairs in Scotland

## *Informal arrangements*

A legal principle (called **negotiorum gestio**) allows you to act on behalf of an incapable person, providing your actions are for her benefit. It applies when it can be assumed that the person would have authorised you if she had been capable. This principle may be useful in an emergency situation, for example when immediate repairs are required to a house and you need to claim back money spent on someone else's behalf. Some organisations may not accept this informal arrangement.

## *Power of attorney*

If the power of attorney was signed after 1 January 1991 it will remain valid after the person giving it becomes mentally incapable. A solicitor will be needed to prepare the power of attorney.

## *Curator bonis*

If your relative has not appointed a power of attorney and is mentally incapable of looking after her affairs or appointing someone else to look after them, then a **curator bonis** may have to be appointed. A curator bonis is an individual appointed by and responsible to the court. Usually a solicitor or accountant is appointed (though not necessarily) and the curator has to manage all the financial affairs and property of the person. The application to the court for a curator bonis to be appointed is prepared by a solicitor, usually on behalf of a close relative of the person. Having a curator appointed is expensive and any professional will charge an annual administration fee. It is therefore not recommended for people with less than £15,000 of capital.

# For more *i*nformation

❶ *Dementia: Money and Legal Matters*, available free to carers from Alzheimer Scotland – Action on Dementia (address on p 95).

*❶* Age Concern Factsheet 22 *Legal Arrangements for Managing Financial Affairs*, available from Age Concern Scotland.

*❶* *Information for Families of Persons Subject to Curatory*, free leaflet from the Accountant of Court (address on p 95).

*❶* *Dementia in the Community*, free leaflet from the Mental Welfare Commission for Scotland, K Floor, Argyle House, 3 Lady Lawson Street, Edinburgh EH3 9SH.

# Making a Will and sorting out your affairs

People vary in how much time they want to spend thinking about legal and practical arrangements before they die. Some people find it satisfying to set their affairs in order, to know that things have been dealt with in the way that they want and to feel that they have provided as well as they can for those they love. Some people want arrangements to be made but prefer to delegate the details to someone else. Others simply find it too painful to think about these things.

If you are close enough, you may feel able to discuss such matters with your relative.

## Making a Will

People sometimes think it is not worth making a Will because they assume that anything they own will automatically go to those closest to them. But if you die without making a Will, or the Will is not valid, or if you have got married or divorced since making the Will, there are strict rules laid down in law about how the estate (your money and property) will be divided. These rules can cause difficulties and sometimes hardship for families. It can mean that people you would like to provide for are not included.

You and your relative could both make a Will if you haven't made one already. Doing this together can help make it easier for your relative, who may find it very painful to think about arrangements after his death.

The Will names one or more people to be the **executors**: they are responsible for sorting out the person's money and property (their 'estate') and carrying out the instructions in the Will. The executor is usually a spouse or other close relative, but it could be a professional such as a solicitor or bank manager. A professional executor will usually charge a fee, which is paid out of the estate.

### Getting help with making a Will

It is often best to ask a solicitor to help in drawing up a Will, especially if your affairs are at all complicated. Solicitors' fees vary a great deal, from about £35 to £200, so it is worth ringing round and asking for a quotation.

Some people draw up their own Wills. The Consumers' Association guide *Wills and Probate* tells you how to do this, and they also produce a Will pack for use in England and Wales. Age Concern England also has a useful factsheet. It is important that the Will is clear, and that it is dated, signed and witnessed in the right way, otherwise it will not be valid. The executor can be a beneficiary (someone who benefits from the Will) but witnesses to the signature and their relatives cannot.

Note  Be careful if you are drawing up your own Will in Scotland. Many of the preprinted forms available are designed for use outside Scotland where the rules are different.

# For more *i*nformation

*i* DSS booklet D 49 *What to Do After a Death*.

*i* Age Concern England Factsheet 7 *Making your Will*.

*i* *Wills and Probate, What to Do When Someone Dies* and their Will pack *Make Your Own Will: A practical guide to making your own Will (England and Wales)*, all published by the Consumers' Association (address on p 99).

*i* *What to Do After a Death in Scotland*, leaflet available free from the Scottish Office Home Department, V1 Spur, Saughton House, Edinburgh EH11 3XD.

51

## Making a 'living will'

Some people have clear views about what treatment they would or would not like to receive in the last stages of a terminal illness. A 'living will' or 'advance directive' is a document which enables someone to state in advance what treatment they would wish to receive or refuse when they are no longer capable of indicating their wishes.

A living will is helpful when difficult decisions about care or treatment have to be made, as it tells doctors and friends or relatives what the ill person's wishes would be. However, people's views about care and treatment often change as they become more ill. If your relative has made a living will, encourage him to review it from time to time and make changes if he wishes.

In England and Wales an advance directive which refuses treatment to prolong life is legally binding on doctors, providing it is clear that the person was fully capable when they made the decision. In Scotland the position regarding advance directives is much less clear.

Not everyone likes the idea of a written document. Some people prefer simply to discuss their wishes confidentially with someone they are close to, and to entrust this person with making their views known at the appropriate time.

# For more *i*nformation

ⓘ *The Natural Death Handbook*, produced by the Natural Death Centre and published by Virgin. Includes sections on making your Will, sorting out your affairs, living wills and dying wishes.

ⓘ Advance directives with accompanying notes are available from the **Voluntary Euthanasia Society**, 13 Prince of Wales Terrace, London W8 5PG. Tel 0171–937 7770.

ⓘ Living Will forms and notes are available from the **Terrence Higgins Trust** (address p 107). These are free of charge to people affected by HIV/AIDS; a donation is appreciated from other enquirers. Please send an A4 size sae.

## Other practical arrangements the ill person may want to consider

■ Making arrangements for the future of children under 18, and appointing guardians in the event of both parents dying.

■ Making a list of important documents (eg Will, marriage certificate, title deeds of the house) and where they are kept, and details of bank or building society accounts, insurance policies, pension schemes, etc.

■ Making a list of people who should be informed of the death (eg solicitor, the person named as executor of the Will).

■ Leaving his body for medical research or organ donation – if your relative would like to do this, the GP or consultant can tell him whether it is possible. Age Concern England Factsheet 27 *Arranging a funeral* explains the procedure.

■ Writing down details of everyday tasks that someone else will need to take over (eg where to get the car serviced, how to light the boiler, how to use the washing machine or start the lawnmower).

■ Making plans for the funeral service, burial or cremation, and wake or gathering after the funeral – not everyone wishes to think about these arrangements, but some people do.

■ Taking out a pre-paid funeral plan – the British Institute of Funeral Directors (address on p 97) can send you a leaflet called *Taking Care of the Future*, which explains how to arrange and pay for a funeral in advance.

■ Reducing his heirs' Inheritance Tax liability. When someone dies Inheritance Tax (IHT) may have to be paid if the value of their estate is above a certain level (£215,000 in 1997–98). Gifts or assets left to a spouse are not included. Some gifts made within seven years of death may also be taxed. It may be possible to reduce any IHT bill by putting money into a trust, perhaps for children or grandchildren. Or unmarried partners might wish to marry. Certain gifts are also exempt from IHT.

## For more *i*nformation

*ⓘ Your Taxes and Savings*, published annually by Age Concern Books (details on p 111).

# 5 Living with the illness

*This chapter looks at the middle stage of terminal illness, at what it means for the person who is ill and for the person giving care. The first part looks at ways of dealing with common symptoms and making the ill person as comfortable as possible. It also discusses going into hospital, either for tests or treatment or to give the person who is caring a break.*

*The second part looks at the emotional effects of being ill both on the ill person and on those who are close to her. The illness brings loss and change for everyone involved. There is no right or wrong way to cope with these changes, but understanding what is happening and being able to talk about it can make it easier to live with the illness, and to find ways of getting on with life and enjoying the best parts of the time that is left.*

## Being ill

'Getting up for a cup of tea or a visit to the bathroom is a major undertaking – you could hardly imagine doing both within an hour of each other.'

'Think for a moment about what it feels like when you get flu. You know the second-day-of-flu feeling when you feel simply rotten, when everything hurts or is uncomfortable and when you can hardly do anything. We have all had that – and felt very sorry for ourselves, but we've also known that the feeling would pass and we would be back to normal in a week.

'Now imagine that this second-day-of-flu feeling does not go away and you are feeling just as bad at the end of a week. Imagine how you would feel at the end of the second week. Then imagine it for a month. A month – you are not back at work, and nobody can tell you when you're going to get back to work. If at all. Now add to that a regular series of tests – X-rays, blood tests, scans – and perhaps treatments with drugs by tablet or injection, or with radiotherapy or surgery. On top of that there may be all the uncertainty about the future …'

Dr Robert Buckman, in his book *I Don't Know What to Say*, describes the feeling of living with a terminal illness as 'the grind'. In the passage quoted above he asks us to imagine how this feels for the person who is ill.

# Dealing with symptoms

As the illness progresses, your relative may move gradually or more rapidly from feeling fairly healthy to feeling ill. Although there may be days or weeks when she feels relatively well, there is likely to come a time when there are continuous physical symptoms due to the illness or the side-effects of treatment.

Symptoms vary according to the illness, and can vary between people with the same illness. Some people become very ill quite quickly, others have few symptoms until the final stages. The same symptoms can affect people differently. Someone who has always been very independent may find it harder to deal with being ill than a person who is more willing to accept support and care from other people.

There is not enough space in this book to discuss all the possible symptoms that can appear in the course of a terminal illness. This section looks at some of the common ones. Most people are likely to experience some of these as the illness progresses, but everyone is different.

There are often things that the ill person or carer can do themselves to help the problem. The doctor or nurse may be able to advise you. National helplines, national organisations and local self-help groups concerned with a particular illness can often give very helpful advice about coping with symptoms. They are used to dealing with all kinds of questions from carers and can make suggestions based on other people's experiences of living with the illness. (See the list of organisations on pp 95–108.)

Note Sometimes people with a terminal illness and those caring for them don't ask for help with symptoms because they assume that they are an inevitable part of the illness and that nothing can be done about them. This is not the case. It is important to tell the hospital doctor, GP or district nurse about any symptom. With the right help, almost all symptoms can be reduced or relieved. If the first course of action doesn't seem to help, tell the doctor or nurse that it isn't working, so that they can try a different approach.

## *Pain*

Although many people are afraid that a terminal illness will mean pain, this is not necessarily the case. Most people believe that cancer causes pain, but one in four people with advanced cancer has no pain at all. Fear can make pain worse, so if your relative is worried, talk to the doctor or nurse. They may be able to reassure her that pain is unlikely or explain how it can be relieved. Today medical knowledge about the control and relief of pain is very sophisticated. If people do experience pain, it can almost always be reduced; often it can be controlled so that it does not come back. People who have had pain often assume that it will return or increase when they are dying, but in most people, pain tends to get less towards the end of life.

If your relative does have persistent pain, it needs to be treated and you should tell the doctor or nurse. The doctor may decide to prescribe stronger medication such as morphine, or a combination of medicines, as the causes of pain may vary. People are often frightened that morphine will be addictive, but this is not the case when it is given for chronic pain. The doctor will probably adjust the dose over several days, and it is important that the medication is taken regularly, following instructions, to prevent the pain from returning. It is likely to cause some drowsiness at first, and sometimes nausea, but this usually disappears after two or three days. Each person's needs differ, and an increasing dose does not mean that the disease is getting worse. If medication doesn't help and the pain is unrelieved, you or your GP could contact the Macmillan Nursing Service. (A hospital or district nurse will be able to tell you if there is a Macmillan nurse in your area or you can contact the Cancer Relief Macmillan Fund – address on p 98.) Macmillan nurses specialise in pain relief. They may give you advice, speak to the GP on your behalf, or suggest that you ask the GP to refer your relative to a doctor who specialises in pain control.

You could also contact your local hospice – get the address from the Hospice Information Service (address on p 102). Hospice doctors are very experienced in pain control and often work with GPs to provide care and pain relief for people being cared for at home.

Other treatments can help to relieve pain, either along with medication or on their own – for example massage, acupuncture, hypnotherapy, aromatherapy, relaxation techniques, TENS (transcutaneous electrical nerve stimulation) and in some cases radiotherapy. The Macmillan nurse or district nurse may be able to advise about complementary treatments and about local practitioners of complementary therapies who may specialise in pain relief.

## Loss of appetite

People who are ill often have little appetite. If your relative is not eating much, encourage her to eat as and when she pleases. Smaller, more frequent meals and tasty snacks are better than large meals. If she finds it an effort to eat because she is too weak, try to make eating as easy and comfortable as possible, with pillows or cushions and a table or tray at the right height. Worrying or putting pressure on her to eat can make the problem more distressing for her.

Your relative may not feel like eating because of a dry or sore mouth. People who are ill tend to get mouth infections more easily, but these can be treated. Using a gentle mouthwash and brushing teeth or dentures regularly can help to keep the mouth moist and reduce the risk of infection.

If your relative needs help with eating and drinking, allow plenty of time to do this so that you are relaxed and not feeling rushed or worried about other things. Give small mouthfuls of food and let her eat at her own pace.

## Nausea or vomiting

Nausea and vomiting may have many causes. Once the doctor has established the cause, symptoms can usually be relieved by prescribing medicines, or changing the prescription if your relative is already taking anti-sickness medication.

## Constipation

Constipation is a common problem when people are ill. It may be caused by loss of appetite, a lack of exercise or medication. Having plenty to drink and increasing the amount of fibre in the diet can help. The doctor may prescribe a laxative to ease the problem. Sometimes the district nurse can insert a suppository in the rectum or back passage to help relieve severe constipation.

## Incontinence (loss of bladder or bowel control)

Loss of bladder or bowel control often happens in the later stages of illness. In the middle stages it may be due to an infection which can be treated. Sometimes loss of bladder control is caused by severe constipation and clears up when this is treated. If your relative begins to lose control of her bladder or bowels, contact the district nurse, who can give you advice and show you how to keep her as comfortable as possible.

District nurses can supply a waterproof sheet for the bed and special pads to keep bedding and clothing dry. If the problem arises because your relative needs to get to the toilet more urgently or frequently but is very weak, the district nurse can arrange the loan of a commode or bedpan.

Some areas have a continence adviser who can assess and give advice about serious problems. There may also be a laundry service. The district nurse will be able to tell you what services are available in your area, or phone the Incontinence Information Helpline on 0191–213 0050.

## Pressure sores

If someone sits or lies in one position for a long time, the skin over the bony parts of the body such as the heels and base of the spine begins to break down, causing pressure sores.

Changing position frequently is the best way to prevent pressure sores. If your relative is able to move about a little then sitting in a chair and lying in bed alternately, or walking round the bed, will help. If she is too weak to move, the district nurse can show you how to change her position regularly and care for her skin. The nurse can also advise about – and sometimes lend – wedge-shaped pillows, a sheepskin or a special soft mattress to help prevent sores.

## Smells

Changing bedding or clothing and emptying a commode or bedpan as soon as possible will help to cut down smells. Sometimes an infection in a wound or in the urine can cause a smell or a smelly discharge. This is not unusual but it can be very upsetting for the person who is ill. The doctor may be able to treat the infection so that the smell is reduced. Perfume, aftershave or scented oils or candles may help to mask smells.

## Confusion

Confusion often occurs in the final stages of a terminal illness, but it sometimes happens earlier than this. It is sometimes caused by an infection, constipation or medication, and it may improve if the infection or constipation is treated or if the medication is changed or stopped. If no specific cause is found, the doctor may be able to prescribe medicines which help.

Becoming confused can be very upsetting for the ill person, who often realises that something is wrong and may be frightened that she is going mad. Family and friends may find it distressing because they don't know how to talk to her or what to do to help. It may help if you can reassure your relative that she is all right in herself, and that it is the illness which makes her do or experience strange things.

A confused person can become very agitated when she wants to do something but is too weak or muddled to do it herself or say what it is she wants. It may be something simple like wanting to go to the toilet, so it is worth asking if this is the problem. If your relative is confused, it may be worth encouraging her to go to the toilet regularly.

### Other problems

Other problems to ask the doctor or nurse about include:

| | |
|---|---|
| indigestion | waterbrash (heartburn) |
| diarrhoea | breathlessness |
| a cough | swelling (oedema) |
| an unpleasant discharge | sleeplessness |
| difficulty in passing urine | sweating |
| hiccoughs | unwanted drowsiness |
| muscle cramps | difficulty with swallowing |

## For more *i*nformation

*ⓘ* *Feeling Better: Controlling pain and other symptoms of cancer*, published by BACUP (address on p 96).

*ⓘ* Age Concern England Factsheet 23 *Help with incontinence*.

*ⓘ* Other national voluntary organisations for specific illnesses also produce information leaflets on dealing with symptoms and other common problems. See list on pages 95–108.

# Going into hospital

## Having tests and treatment

During the middle phase of a terminal illness, the person who is ill may be cared for most of the time at home by the GP. At some point she may need to go into hospital for tests or treatment or the relief of symptoms. This might be for a short or a longer stay. It might only happen once, or occasionally. If the ill person needs chemotherapy or radiotherapy it may in some cases become a regular routine. Or she may have to make regular visits for checkups, tests or treatment on an outpatient basis.

People often feel very apprehensive in the days before a stay in hospital or an outpatient visit, especially if they are not sure what to expect. Your relative may be noticeably depressed or irritable towards other people. You can help by getting as much information as possible about what is going to happen, and by encouraging her to talk about how she is feeling.

■ Does your relative know what the test or treatment is for?
■ Do you need more information about what it involves, or about how she is likely to feel afterwards?
■ Do you and your relative want an opportunity to ask questions or discuss the benefits and disadvantages of the treatment with the doctor?
■ Does your relative need more time to make a decision?
■ Does she need someone to talk to about her feelings and fears about treatment?

There are more suggestions about questions you may want to ask about treatment on page 17.

## Preparing for a hospital visit

A hospital stay can mean a break from the routine of caring, but it can also be stressful if you are worried about your relative or if the hospital is some way away or difficult to get to. Daily visiting becomes very tiring and can be expensive over a long period.

61

If your relative is weak she may sleep a lot, but if she is awake for most of the day, she may find that boredom is a problem. With nothing to do but think about being ill, some people become depressed or withdrawn. See below for suggestions about people who may be able to visit and give support.

There may be some things you can organise in advance to make a stay in hospital as easy as possible for both of you.

### Checklist for going into hospital

*Visiting arrangements*

■ Can you rearrange your daily routine around visiting, instead of trying to fit visiting in with what you normally do?

■ Can you get help with routine tasks like shopping or collecting children from school to give you more time for visiting?

■ If you have to travel a long distance, or if you are at work during visiting hours, can you arrange a different visiting time?

■ Are volunteer drivers available if you have no means of transport (ask the person in charge of the ward or the hospital welfare officer)?

*Money*

■ Will your relative's benefits be affected (see DSS leaflet NI 9 *Going into Hospital?*)?

■ Will she need help with the cost of transport (see p 44)?

*Things to take*

■ Pack an extra dressing gown, nightie or pyjamas so that you can take spare ones home to wash.

■ Pack or take in things to relieve boredom – books, magazines, personal stereo with music or talking tapes, pen, writing paper or notebook, change for telephone.

■ If your relative is confused, label her possessions clearly so that they don't get lost.

*People who may be able to visit and give support to someone in hospital*

■ Hospital chaplain.

■ Hospital social worker.
■ Macmillan nurse.
■ Hospital volunteer visitors.
■ Someone from a local self-help group concerned with the illness.
■ Patient advocate, interpreter or link worker, if your relative's first language is not English.

## Respite care to give the carer a break

If your relative needs a lot of care, or if you have been caring for some time, it may be possible to arrange for her to have a short stay in a hospital, hospice or nursing home so that you can get a break, for anything from a few days to a couple of weeks. Although it may be hard to think about leaving your relative in the care of someone else, a good respite care arrangement often makes it possible to continue caring at home for longer. It can also give your relative the chance to get to know the doctors and nurses who will care for her if she needs to be admitted in the final stage of the illness. The chart on pages 23–24 describes some alternative forms of care and how to find out more about them. Normally respite care is arranged through the GP or social services department.

# The emotional effects of being ill

Being ill affects everyone – the sick person, the person who is caring for her, and other members of the family and close friends. For everyone it means the loss of a 'normal' life.

## The feelings of the person who is ill

### Tom

'I think it's what it must be like walking up to the gallows. You know it's certain that you're going to die, but you still keep hoping that someone's going to arrive with a reprieve.'

In learning to live with the illness there is often a middle stage in the kinds of feelings that people experience. This may or may not correspond to a middle stage in the progress of the physical illness.

Chapter 1 looked at denial, anger and some of the other feelings which are common in the early stages of illness. As the sick person increasingly feels the physical effects of the illness and begins to realise that the symptoms are not going to go away, other feelings often take the place of these earlier ones. She may feel very isolated even though she is surrounded by sympathetic and supportive relatives and friends. She may experience a gradual loss of hope and descent into depression, or swing violently between hope and despair, or move backwards and forwards between these reactions. She may be fearful about how the illness will develop, about pain, about dying, about what will happen to those she loves after her death.

People react in different ways to living with uncertainty. Some people have a strong sense of 'entering a tunnel' or 'closing down' as the illness progresses, and deal with this by wanting to set their affairs in order. Others prefer to try and live as much as possible in the present, and choose not to know or think about the uncertainties of the future.

### An adjustment of hope

As someone adjusts to being ill, there is often an adjustment of hope. Many people go through a phase of 'bargaining' where they begin to adjust their goals and expectations: 'If we can go on holiday this summer, I won't mind so much what happens after that.' Carers often go through a phase of bargaining too, sometimes on behalf of the person they care for and sometimes for themselves. People say things like, 'If she can last until her grandchild's born, I know she will be happy', or 'If I could only have him home from hospital for Christmas, I'll at least have that to remember'.

### Depression and despair

The other side of this adjustment is a loss of hope. Your relative may find herself wondering whether it is worth buying new clothes or planning a holiday. She may decide to cancel a subscription or a holiday because she sees no point in planning for something when she doesn't know if she is going to be there to enjoy it.

A person who is ill needs hope – in order to keep going, but at the same time, if the hopes are to be realistic, she needs to begin to accept that death is inevitable. This emotional balancing act can be stressful and exhausting, and there is no easy solution. You can play an important part by encouraging your relative to talk about her feelings and to focus on hopes that are realistic and achievable.

# How you can help

- Show your relative that you realise how low she feels – don't rush in with advice or rush away to do something else. Remember that just being there helps – sometimes there is nothing you can say.
- Don't encourage false hopes.
- Talk about realistic hopes and goals. These will vary – what is realistic for one person may not be realistic for another.

Depending on how she is feeling, it may help to encourage your relative to think along the lines of one of the questions below:

- What do I want to do that will make it worth getting out of bed today?
- What do I want to keep going for? What is worth aiming for?
- What do I want to do before I die?

Page 71 gives some suggestions about things that people sometimes hope to be able to do when they know that death is approaching. These ideas may suggest a starting point for you to talk to your relative about her own personal wishes and hopes.

### Getting help for depression

If your relative is feeling very depressed or despairing, she may find it helpful to talk to a trained counsellor. The GP, Macmillan nurse or medical social worker (attached to the GP's surgery or health centre) may be able to offer counselling or put you in touch with a suitable counsellor. The GP may refer your relative to a psychologist or psychiatrist who specialises in working with people who are dying, or prescribe medication which can help to relieve overwhelming feelings of depression or despair.

## The feelings of the carer

This middle phase of illness and uncertainty means an emotional balancing act for the carer as well as the ill person, and it is often very wearing. As carer you will have to make an adjustment of your own hopes and expectations, as well as giving practical care and emotional support to your relative. Often you will be the one who bears the brunt of your relative's anger, frustration and resentment, who has to cope with her depression or withdrawal.

Illness usually means that the carer has to take on some of the roles and responsibilities that the ill person can no longer manage alone – perhaps cooking, or handling the household finances. This can be difficult for both of you. Your relative may find it distressing that she can no longer cope on her own. You may find it hard to accept your relative's increasing dependence. Sometimes the carer has to help with intimate personal care. Coping with conditions such as incontinence can be difficult for both the ill person and the carer.

As the illness progresses your relative is likely to become more dependent on other people for the help and care that she needs. If the illness causes a loss of physical or mental faculties, it may begin to alter her behaviour or personality. This is distressing in itself, but it is often made worse by uncertainty about how long it will go on for. If the illness is a long one many carers begin to feel worn down by the daily demands of caring, and feelings of frustration and resentment are very common.

Caring for someone often means that the main carer has less time to spend with other members of the family. It may mean that a spouse, partner or children have to take on extra responsibilities, or help with looking after the ill person. All this can put a tremendous strain on families, and even the strongest families can begin to suffer.

### *What you can do*

■ Look after yourself and your own health. To cope with caring over a long period the minimum you need is enough sleep and rest, a regular break from caring, and support from other people. If you are not getting this basic minimum, talk to the GP, nurse or social worker about getting more help.

■ Try to make some regular time for yourselves as a family, away from the person you care for. Try to talk openly to the rest of the family about the situation, and how each of you feels about it. If caring is beginning to put a severe strain on family relationships, you may need to think about alternative forms of care (see p 23).

■ Be flexible. Get information about alternative forms of care and be prepared to change your plans. If it becomes necessary to give intimate personal care, such as help with incontinence, but you or your relative feels unable to cope with this, contact the district nurse. It may be possible to arrange for someone else to help.

■ Think ahead. Things may reach a point where you can no longer care for your relative at home. You will feel happier if you have planned for this in advance, rather than having to make snap decisions when a crisis occurs.

## For more *i*nformation

ⓘ *I Don't Know What to Say: How to help and support someone who is dying* by Robert Buckman, published by Papermac. Offers sympathetic insight into the feelings of patients and carers, and advice on giving emotional support. It is now out of print but worth getting hold of through your public library.

ⓘ *Caring at Home When Cancer Cannot be Cured*, a short booklet for carers published by CancerLink (address on p 98).

ⓘ *Coping at Home: Caring for someone with advanced cancer*, published by BACUP (address on p 96).

ⓘ *Facing the Challenge of Advanced Cancer*, a short booklet for people with cancer published by BACUP (address on p 96).

**ⓘ** *The Natural Death Handbook,* produced by the Natural Death Centre and published by Virgin. Includes a helpful chapter on 'Practical care for the dying', which covers the physical and emotional needs of the ill person and carer.

# 6 Approaching death

*In the final stage of a terminal illness the person who is ill may begin to realise from the changes in his body that he is dying: death is no longer an uncertain event in the future. In this stage some people are able to accept that death is inevitable. Some are never able to accept that they are dying. Sometimes the ill person and carer are at different stages of acceptance.*

*This chapter looks at how the person who is caring can help and support someone in the final stages of illness. It discusses the needs and feelings both of the person who is dying and of family members and friends as death approaches.*

*It is always difficult to predict when death will come, but there is often a noticeable change in the sick person when death is near. The last part of this chapter describes how to recognise when death is approaching, and what practical help and support the doctor or district nurse can give if you are caring for a dying person at home.*

## Jenny

'I'm glad he wasn't on his own at the end – they were both there. It comforts me to know that.'

'My brother had been in hospital about a week and my sister-in-law was spending most of the day with him. The hospital phoned her at about ten o'clock one night to say that my brother probably wouldn't last the night. She was at home on her own and phoned me in a dreadful state because there was no way to get to the hospital except by taxi and she had hardly any money. I said I would drive over and fetch her and I phoned her daughter who said she would drive down. When we got to the hospital my brother was unconscious. We sat with him until my niece arrived at about one in the morning. The nurses offered us a camp bed. My sister-in-law was absolutely exhausted by this point, and my niece more or less ordered her to go home. She stayed with him that night and the next night, and looked after my sister-in-law during the day. My brother died three days later. He wasn't conscious during that time but I think he was fighting until the end. I remember thinking he died in the way that he'd lived, stubborn to the end. I'm glad he wasn't on his own at the end – they were both there. It comforts me to know that.'

# Understanding the needs of the person who is dying

None of us can fully understand the feelings of someone who is dying until we go through it ourselves. Most people find it very difficult to know how to help and support someone who is facing death. It may help to try and think about how you might feel if you were in the ill person's place. Try asking yourself the question, 'What would I like to do if I had only three months to live?'

This is a painful question to think about, and there are no right or wrong answers. People have different priorities, and yours may be very different from those of the person you care for. These are some of the things that often seem important to people who are approaching death:

- having the chance to say goodbye to the people they love and care for;

■ setting their affairs in order so that everything is easy to sort out after their death;

■ knowing that their family will be financially secure and able to cope without them;

■ dying peacefully, without pain;

■ knowing that someone will be with them when they die;

■ feeling that they won't be forgotten after their death.

## How you can help

You may find it very difficult to talk to your relative about these things, but there are nevertheless ways in which you may be able to help.

■ There may be things you would like to say to each other – it is sometimes difficult to know how to start, but it will help both of you if you try.

■ There may be other people that the ill person would like to say goodbye to.

■ Your relative may want to talk about his fears, or about what it is like to die. The next section discusses some common fears about dying and how you may be able to help.

■ You may want to tell your relative in your own way that he will not be forgotten, and to talk about how you and other people will remember him.

■ You may be able to help him to set his affairs in order, as discussed on pages 50–53. For some people, discussing practical arrangements and tidying up their affairs helps bring peace of mind.

# Fears about dying

We are all afraid of dying, and almost everyone goes through a period of being afraid during a terminal illness. For some people this happens at an early stage in the illness. For others, this kind of fear may surface or become more difficult to ignore as the illness progresses. People are often afraid that the anxiety – sometimes panic – that they feel in the early stages will increase as

71

the illness advances, but often these fears lessen as the ill person slowly adjusts and learns to live with the illness. Increasing weakness often brings an increasing sense of resignation, and sometimes peacefulness and acceptance.

It is not cowardly to be afraid of dying. It is part of our natural instinct for self-preservation. But because we live in a society where dying and death are outside most people's experience, it is very difficult to acknowledge these feelings, let alone to put them into words. It is also very difficult to listen and give comfort to someone who is afraid of dying.

## How you can help

Often just talking about these fears, perhaps with a relative or friend, or with a sympathetic doctor or nurse, can be comforting for a person who is approaching death.

The important thing is to give your relative plenty of opportunity to talk about how he is feeling and what he is worried about. If he starts to say how low or awful he is feeling, encourage him to say more. Don't stop him talking or change the subject. If you find it difficult to know what to say, say so. Most people do. Just being prepared to listen shows that you care; it is better than leaving him to face his fear alone.

If you are not sure how to reassure your relative yourself, you or he may find it helpful to talk to the doctor or nurse. If they have a lot of experience of caring for people who are dying, they will understand these fears. They may be able to reassure your relative that what he fears is unlikely to happen, or find a way of helping him to come to terms with his fear.

### Fear of pain

Pain is perhaps the thing that people fear most about a terminal illness, especially cancer. The fear of 'dying in agony' is a common one, but this is not what normally happens at the end of a long illness. It may help to ask the doctor or nurse about this – they can give your relative more information about how his illness will progress and whether he is likely to have any pain. They may be able to reassure him, or explain what can be done to control and relieve pain if it should occur. There is more information about pain relief on pages 56–57.

## Fear of 'ceasing to be'

Most of us find it impossible to believe that we will cease to be. Some people reach a kind of acceptance or peacefulness when death is near, but others never do.

For some people the fear of death is related to a spiritual questioning or doubt about what happens after death. People who are religious sometimes find it very hard to deal with fear if they believe their faith should give them strength. They may find it helpful to talk to a priest who has experience of caring for people who are dying.

For others fear of death may be the simple but powerful fear of the unknown.

## Fear of choking or suffocation

Death at the end of a terminal illness is generally peaceful, and people do not usually choke to death or suffocate, but this is a common fear, especially if the illness affects the lungs, chest or throat. The doctor or nurse may be able to reassure your relative that the illness will not cause death in this way.

## Fear of losing control

Many people are afraid of losing control over their lives. As children we are taught to strive for independence, which is closely tied up with our self-esteem and dignity. Being ill and dependent on other people can seem like losing control and dignity. It may be well-meaning to want to do everything for someone who is ill, but it may make them feel that they are losing control when this is not necessary. You may help your relative by enabling him to make decisions and remain independent for as long as possible – for example, he may want to continue making out the shopping list long after he is too weak to go to the shops himself.

## Fear of being buried or cremated alive

This is a common anxiety, which may perhaps stem from the difficulty we all have in thinking about or imagining ourselves as dead. It may help your relative to reassure him that this is a fear which tends to fade as the illness progresses and his own feelings and changes in his body tell him that death is approaching.

## Fear of being useless or of being a burden

Many people go through a phase of asking themselves, 'What's the point in going on?' This question can cover a whole range of feelings. It shouldn't be brushed aside – someone who is feeling like this needs to be listened to, and needs to talk about the feelings of emptiness or despair that lie behind the question.

Sometimes people with a terminal illness feel useless because it is so hard to accept that the illness limits what they can do. Their fear of growing limitations in the future may prevent them from enjoying what they can do in the present.

Sometimes people are afraid of being a burden on those who care for them. It may help to ask your relative how he would feel if it were the other way round: would he regard it as a burden to care for you? He may need reassuring that through his life he has earned the care he is receiving. It may help to point out that he is giving relatives or friends an important chance to return the care and love that they have received over the years.

## Fear of separation, sudden death or being alone

Some psychologists suggest that we all experience anxiety at the thought of being separated by our death from those we love, just as a baby or small child feels anxious at being separated from its mother. People are often afraid that they will die suddenly, or at night, when no one else is there. It may help if you can reassure your relative that there is usually some warning when death is near, that someone will be there with him, that he will not be left to die alone.

If someone is being cared for in hospital or in a hospice when death is expected, relatives or friends often make arrangements for someone to be there all the time. Most hospitals and hospices are happy to provide an armchair or camp bed and blankets so that a relative or friend can stay with the dying person through the night.

# The dying person's wishes about care in the final stage

Some people have very specific wishes about how they would like to be cared for in their last days and hours; they may discuss these with those who care for them or perhaps make a living will, as described on page 52. If your relative has specific wishes, ask to discuss these with the doctor at an appropriate point.

Other people find these questions too painful to consider or talk about. If you are not able to discuss these things with your relative, you may have to make decisions on his behalf. These are some of the questions you may need to consider.

## Where does your relative want to die?

Most people prefer the idea of dying at home, and you may feel that you would like to care for your relative at home if this is what he wants. But it is important to balance the wishes of the dying person with his need for care and the needs of other family members.

Sometimes there is a deterioration in the ill person which makes it difficult to provide the necessary care at home. The doctor or nurse may suggest that the quality of the time remaining to your relative would be better if he was admitted to hospital.

Some people are afraid that they will not be able to cope with caring for a dying person, or anxious about how they will react to death. These are very natural fears. Discussing them with the doctor or nurse can help to reassure the person giving care that they will not have to cope alone, and that there is enough support and practical help available. Sometimes it is the right decision not to care at home, and to make arrangements for admission to hospital in advance.

If the ill person has spent time in hospital or a hospice during the illness and built up a good relationship with the doctors and nurses, he may feel more secure there where there is round-the-clock nursing care and pain or other symptoms can be promptly relieved.

Being cared for in hospital or a hospice often means that family and friends have more time just to be with the dying person, without the worry and strain of giving practical care 24 hours a day.

## Would he like a priest of his religion or the last rites?

If you are not sure, and you feel able to bring up the subject, it may be worth asking your relative about this. Even someone who has not been strongly religious in life might wish to have a priest called or the last rites said when death is near.

Hospital and hospice nursing staff will do their best to meet the spiritual needs of the dying person and their family. If your relative belongs to a religion that nurses may be unfamiliar with, it will be helpful to discuss with them how to contact the appropriate minister of religion, or who should say the last rites, and anything else that will help them to meet your relative's wishes.

## Are there any specific instructions about washing or laying out his body?

Normally a hospital nurse, district nurse or undertaker will see to this, but sometimes relatives or friends like to do it themselves, or to help in the task. If your relative's religion requires specific instructions to be followed, it is a good idea to make sure that the nurses are aware of these before he dies, so that nothing is done which might go against his wishes or cause distress to relatives.

# How will I know when death is near?

Carers sometimes feel anxious that they will not know when death is approaching, or that they will not be there at the moment of death. Some people are afraid that they will lose control or panic, or that death will be frightening.

It is never possible to predict exactly when death will come, and there is no set pattern to events in the last days and hours. But death at the end of an illness is usually quite peaceful, not sudden, violent or painful. Most people are not conscious at the moment of death. In the final stages the dying person often becomes increasingly drowsy before slipping into a period of unconsciousness which may last hours or even days.

If your relative is in hospital or a hospice and you would like to be called when death is near, tell the nursing staff and they will make sure that you are telephoned.

If you are looking after your relative at home, there are usually some warning signs that death is approaching. He may become noticeably weaker or drowsy. He may become so weak or drowsy that he is no longer able to eat or drink, but he will be unaware of either hunger or thirst at this stage. His mouth may be dry, but can be moistened with a damp cloth or sponge. Lip salve will prevent the discomfort of dry, cracked lips. He may lose control of the bladder or bowels.

Contact the nurse and doctor if you think there has been a significant change. Don't feel that you have to cope on your own. They are there to give you advice and support, and the nurse may be able to visit more often or spend more time with you in the last days or hours. They can also provide practical help and care to keep your relative as comfortable as possible.

If the sick person has been taking medicines by mouth, it may be possible to give these by injection or as suppositories. Sometimes a small battery operated pump called a syringe driver is used to give a continuous injection into a vein on the wrist or hand. This is easier and gentler than giving injections every few hours.

Sometimes fluid can build up in the air passages as breathing becomes more shallow. This can make the breathing sound very noisy, though it does not usually cause any distress to the dying person. The doctor may be able to give an injection to dry up the fluid.

Even when someone appears to be unconscious, they may still be able to hear. Other people may need to be reminded not to say anything which your relative would find distressing. It may be comforting if you are able to talk quietly and gently to him and hold his hand, or perhaps stroke his head or put your arms round him – whatever feels most natural.

## Joe

'It was much more peaceful than I expected. She seemed to fade away – I could hear her breathing getting shallower and shallower. Most of the family were there and we took it in turns to sit with her. I was sitting holding her hand when she died. She looked very peaceful. I just sat there for about 15 minutes after she died, still holding her hand and talking to her and crying. But the way it happened seemed so much calmer and more natural than I'd expected.'

## Parveen

'You think you're prepared because you've been expecting it, but you're not. Mum's last few days were very painful for the family. She seemed to be struggling for so long, even though the nurses said she was unconscious. The doctor said, "It's easier for the person doing the dying than for the people watching – she doesn't know anything about it", but I didn't believe that. I don't know if he did, or if he just said it to make us feel better. It took my father a long time to stop remembering those last 24 hours, and to get back his memories of Mum when she was whole and healthy and happy.'

# 7 What to do when someone dies

*If your relative dies in hospital or in a hospice, the staff will take care of some of the practical arrangements and give you advice about what to do. If she dies at home, you may not have had much time to think about practical arrangements in the period before her death. People often feel a sense of panic because they feel they ought to be doing something but have no idea what. This chapter gives a step-by-step guide to the arrangements you will need to make when the person you care for dies.*

## Maria

'It's a bit like trying to find your way out of a maze when you've been hit over the head with a sledgehammer.'

'My mother died in hospital, so there were the nurses who we could ask about what we had to do, but you have this feeling like being in a tunnel or inside a bubble and everyone else is outside, and normal, and you just can't take in what they're saying, or concentrate on anything. When I think back now it all seems a complete jumble, but there's a lot to do in the first few days, and you feel like you're running round doing things all the time, but you can't remember exactly what you did when, or which bit of paper you took where. It's a bit like trying to find your way out of a maze when you've been hit over the head with a sledgehammer.'

'People are very helpful – the hospital welfare officer told me the names of two funeral directors near us, and my neighbour had used one of them and so we chose them. We phoned to get a price first, and then they sent it all in writing, but they were incredibly helpful on the phone and went through all the things that we needed to sort out. They contacted the hospice chaplain to do the service – Mum never went to church but she had met the hospice chaplain at the day centre, so it was nice that there was a connection.

'My husband had the baby a lot of the time but I remember taking her with me to the registrar's office to register the death. I phoned the registrar's office to check everything I needed to take, and the woman there was really helpful too. She went over it all twice and I wrote it down, but I kept putting down the medical certificate and forgetting where I'd put it. Apparently everybody does it – you can't concentrate or remember anything. It didn't really help taking a hungry baby to the registrar's.

'It was dreadful going to the funeral director's to discuss the arrangements. I remember we parked the car and had to walk up a really busy street and I thought at one point my brother was going to faint. It's funny the things that stay in your mind. It was about 200 yards and it was the longest walk of my life. It just happened that that was the point where it really got to my brother – he could hardly speak while we were at the funeral director's.

'Mum was cremated, and the funeral director asked if we wanted them to keep the ashes for us for a little while. They delivered them to the house when we asked for them. It sounds funny when you talk about it, but it was nice to do it like that. We weren't in a state to bring her ashes home in the first week. We spread them in the woodland at the top of a hill where Mum used to take us for picnics when we were kids. Some of my friends think that's weird, but I go up there and look at the view and think of Mum. I think it's a lovely place for her to be.'

# Things to do at once

## 1 Give yourself a little time

Before you do anything else, you may want to just sit down quietly and give yourself time to gather your thoughts. There is no 'right' or 'wrong' way to feel at this moment – people have very different reactions. Some people like to be alone with the dead person for a little while but others do not. Some people feel overwhelmed with feelings of sadness and grief, some feel drained of emotion, some feel dazed or numb. All these reactions are normal and natural.

## 2 Call the doctor

If the GP has been looking after your relative through her illness and knows the cause of death, he or she will confirm that she has died and issue a medical certificate giving the cause of death. You must give this to the registrar when you go to register the death (see point 8 below). The GP should also give you a leaflet explaining how to register the death.

If your relative is to be cremated, you will need an extra form signed by a different doctor. The funeral director or the GP will arrange this.

If the doctor has not seen your relative in the last 14 days, or would like to know more about the cause of death, he or she will report the death to the coroner. The coroner may then arrange for a **post mortem** examination. This usually happens when a person has died from an unknown cause, from an accident or injury, or from an industrial disease. The coroner may also order a post mortem if the person died during an operation or under anaesthetic. There is nothing to be worried about, and there should be no delay in the funeral arrangements. (In Scotland there are no coroners and these functions are carried out by the procurator fiscal.)

## 3 If your relative wanted to be an organ donor

If your relative discussed organ donation with you or carried an organ donor card, contact the nearest hospital as soon as you can so that the organs can be removed quickly. If she dies in a hospital or hospice, tell the doctor or ward sister, who can help to make the necessary arrangements.

## 4 Washing and laying out the person who has died

You may like to wash your relative and perhaps dress her in clean clothes, or help the nurse do this if she or he is with you at the time of death. You do not have to do this – many people prefer a nurse or undertaker to see to it.

## 5 Contact a funeral director

Once you have the medical certificate from the doctor, you can contact a funeral director. The funeral director can give a lot of practical help and guide you through the arrangements. Decisions to be made include:

- Will your relative be buried or cremated? There are some extra forms to be filled in if a person is to be cremated. The funeral director will tell you about these.
- Would you like the body to be kept at home or in a chapel of rest until the funeral?
- Will there be a funeral service or other non-religious ceremony? (If so, you need to contact the people involved – see point 7.)
- Would you prefer people to send flowers or make donations to a charity?

Choose a funeral director who is a member of the British Institute of Funeral Directors or the National Association of Funeral Directors (addresses on pp 97 and 104). You can look up local funeral directors in the *Yellow Pages*, or ask friends and neighbours whom they would recommend. The district nurse or hospital or hospice staff may also be able to suggest some names.

Note If your relative has a pre-paid funeral plan (see p 53), contact the company who issued the plan to find out whether you must go to a named funeral director.

Funerals can be very expensive, so phone round and ask for estimates before you finally decide. The difference between estimates can be several hundred pounds. Make sure you are clear what is included and what is extra and ask for an estimate in writing from the firm that you finally choose.

People who are on a low income may be able to get help with the cost of a funeral from the Social Fund (see p 44).

# For more *i*nformation

- ❶ Age Concern England Factsheet 27 *Arranging a funeral*.
- ❶ *The Natural Death Handbook*, produced by the Natural Death Centre and published by Virgin. Includes a 'Good funeral guide'.

## 6 Contact close relatives and friends

It is a good idea to contact relatives and friends as soon as possible. They will want to give you comfort and support, and they may be able to help you with some of the arrangements.

## 7 Contact a minister of religion or non-religious organisation

If your relative belonged to a religion then contact the minister. Even if she did not attend a place of worship, she may have wanted a religious funeral. If you don't know an appropriate minister, the funeral director or hospital or hospice chaplain may be able to help.

If you want a non-religious ceremony, a society such as the British Humanist Association or the National Secular Society (addresses on pp 97 and 104) may be able to arrange for someone to conduct one, or they can send a form of words that could be used.

# Things to do over the next few days

## 8 Register the death

When someone dies, their death must be registered with the Registrar of Births, Deaths and Marriages for your area within five days. You will find the address in the local telephone directory.

You should show the registrar:

- the medical certificate given you by the GP;
- the pink form (Form 100) given you by the coroner (if the death was reported to the coroner);
- your relative's medical card and war pension order book, if she had one.

The registrar will also want to know:

- your relative's full name, and her maiden name if it was different;
- the date and place of death;
- her last permanent address;
- where and when she was born;
- what her occupation was;
- whether she was receiving a State Pension or other benefits;
- if she was married, the date of birth of the surviving spouse.

The registrar should give you:

- a green certificate for burial or cremation. You should give this to the funeral director: burial or cremation cannot take place without it;
- a white certificate of registration of death, used for claiming social security benefits.

If there is a surviving widow, she should also obtain information leaflets about widows' benefits and Income Tax from the registrar's office.

# For more *i*nformation

❶ DSS Booklet FB 29 *Help When Someone Dies*, for information about all the benefits and allowances you may be entitled to.

The registrar will give you a death certificate only if you ask for one. There is a small charge for this. You may need a death certificate for sorting out the Will, or to claim pension and insurance rights.

### *Registering a death in Scotland*

In Scotland, a death must be registered within eight days, and it may be registered in the registration office for the district in which the death occurred or in the office for the district where the deceased normally lived (as long as this was in Scotland). The information required by a registrar in Scotland is much the same as in England and Wales with some additional questions about the time of death and other family members. After registration the registrar issues a certificate of registration of death which should be given to the funeral director to give to the keeper of the burial ground or to the crematorium. You will also be given a certificate for use in claiming social security benefits. These are both free.

# For more *i*nformation

❶ *What to Do After a Death in Scotland*, free leaflet from the Scottish Office Home Department, V1 Spur, Saughton House, Edinburgh EH11 3XD.

## 9 Sort out the Will

The person named in the Will as the executor is the person responsible for dealing with the money and possessions of the person who has died and distributing them in accordance with the Will. If you are the executor and you feel unable to handle this on your own, you may find it helpful to go to a solicitor or the Citizens Advice Bureau.

Unless the estate is very small, the executor must obtain a **grant of probate** from the Probate Registry office (listed in your local telephone directory) in order to carry out the instructions in the Will. People often pay a solicitor to do this on their behalf, but if the dead person's affairs are not complicated, it is possible to obtain probate without a solicitor's help. In Scotland, this process is called **confirmation** and the executor should apply to the sheriff court.

If there is no Will, someone (usually the nearest relative) must act as the **personal representative** of the person who has died and obtain **letters of administration** from the Probate Registry office instead. In Scotland, if there is no Will, the next of kin may have to apply to the local sheriff court to be appointed as **executor dative**.

# For more *i*nformation

ℹ️ Age Concern England Factsheet 14 *Probate: Dealing with someone else's estate*.

ℹ️ DSS leaflet *How to Obtain Probate*, available from the Registrar of Births, Deaths and Marriages.

ℹ️ *Wills and Probate*, published by the Consumers' Association (address on p 99).

## 10 Return personal documents and NHS equipment

Personal documents such as pension book, passport, driving licence, cheque book and credit cards should be returned to the offices which issued them.

Don't forget to return any NHS equipment on loan to your relative, such as a wheelchair, commode or hearing aid.

## 11 Dispose of personal belongings

Some people find it very distressing to sort through and dispose of the belongings of someone who has died. If possible, do this with other family members or close friends. You will be able to share your memories of your relative and you are less likely to throw away a memento which someone else would have treasured.

Many charities are pleased to accept the personal belongings of someone who has died, or you may like to give them away to family and friends. Some firms specialise in clearing out the homes of people who have died. Look in the local newspapers in the 'Wanted' section. If your relative has any items that are valuable, you may want to keep these and sell them separately.

## For more *i*nformation

*i* DSS booklet D 49 *What to Do After a Death.*

*i* *What to Do When Someone Dies,* published by the Consumers' Association (address on p 99).

# 8 Bereavement and grief

*This chapter discusses the feelings that you may experience after the death of someone you love. Grief is the natural process of adjusting to a major loss, and feelings of grief may last from months to years. It takes most people a year or two to recover from the death of someone who was very important to them. This chapter looks at the many different forms that grief can take, and the various sources of support for people going through bereavement and grief.*

## Ann

'Now, looking back, I think I just went numb, but I didn't realise it. I didn't really start to cry until three or four days after he died.'

'During the last two days when we knew my father was going to die very soon I felt very sad, but I couldn't cry. I was with him when he died and I cried then but I remember the first overwhelming feeling was one of relief. It's as if you're in limbo when you know someone is going to die – there's absolutely nothing you can do but try and hold yourself together.

'Now, looking back, I think I just went numb, but I didn't realise it. I didn't really start to cry until three or four days after he died. My mother was in quite a state and I wasn't trying to be stoical but I think one part of my mind decided to just shut down until it was safe to let go. My mother went through a phase of being very angry – at everything – but I didn't feel that. Just terribly sad and empty.

'For about six months afterwards I felt very raw – I had no self-confidence – even small problems got on top of me. Unexpected things would start me crying – stories on the news about somebody dying, or a game of rugby on TV because he used to love rugby when he was younger. Gradually it got less painful when I thought about him.'

# The stages of grief

There is a pattern in the feelings people experience when someone close to them dies, although people vary widely in the way they cope with their feelings, in how they feel at different stages, and in the time they need to grieve. Knowing what to expect, and knowing that these feelings are shared by other people, may help to reassure you that your own feelings, however painful, are natural and normal.

## Feelings at the time of death

### Pat

'I woke up the day after he died and it just hit me – the neverness of it.'

If your relative had been ill for a long time and his death was expected, you may have felt that you were prepared for death. But the feelings of sadness and grief may be no less intense when it actually happens. The feelings of grief that often follow the diagnosis of a terminal illness mark the beginning of a process of separation from the person who is dying, but the final stage of separation is still the most painful.

For many people it takes time for reality to sink in. You may at first feel exhausted and emotionally drained, especially if you have been caring for a long time. Or you may feel numb or dazed – as though your feelings have closed down. It may take time for feelings of loss and sadness to come to the surface.

You may find that death brings a sense of relief, especially if your relative was so weakened and altered by the illness that the end of his life was a struggle, or if the illness was a long one or if the strain of caring was especially great in the final stages. Not everyone feels this, but you should not feel guilty if you do.

If your relative was very altered by his illness, or if at the end he was very uncomfortable or in pain, these memories can remain very vivid after death, so that it seems difficult at first to think about anything else. It may be difficult to stop going over and over the last days or hours in your head. When you are so close to it, it can seem as though the end of someone's life is all the meaning it has. These kinds of feelings can be very painful, but as time passes recent memories of the illness begin to fade. It becomes easier to replace these with memories of your relative when he was whole and healthy, and of the loving and happy times in your relationship.

## The early stages of grief

Not everyone is the same, but many people experience some of these feelings in the early stages of grief:

**Anxiety** The death of someone close to us overturns our sense of security, the daily routine and 'normal life' – many people go through a phase of intense anxiety until they gradually build up a new routine.

**Great need to cry** Crying is a natural way of releasing intense feelings. Although not everyone wants to express their feelings openly, it is important to recognise them; denying them or bottling them up can be very painful.

**Agitation** It is not unusual to feel restless or agitated, either unable to concentrate or settle to anything or constantly needing something to do; people often experience sudden swings and changes in mood.

**Anger** This is a common reaction and it may be directed at the person who has died for leaving the person who loves them behind, at other members of the family, or at the professionals involved for not doing more to prevent the person from dying; people who are religious sometimes feel angry at God for allowing the ill person to die.

**Guilt** Sometimes anger and the need to blame someone can be turned inward – people often feel guilty that they did not do enough for the ill person, or about things they said or would like to have said before they died.

All these feelings are normal reactions to the pain of loss. Although some of them are more common in the early stages, everyone's experience is different. Sometimes feelings recur even when you feel you have already dealt with them.

## The physical effects of grief

Grief affects many people physically as well as emotionally, especially in the early stages. These are common symptoms:

- loss of appetite, indigestion or an upset stomach, diarrhoea or constipation;
- difficulty in getting to sleep, disturbed sleep and restlessness, or sleeping too long;
- palpitations;
- weight loss.

Any physical symptoms can be upsetting but they usually ease or fade as time passes. Sometimes people experience symptoms which seem similar to those of the person who has died. If this happens talk to your GP, who should be able to reassure you.

## The later stages of grief

Many people go through a phase of depression, often after the intense feelings of the early stages have begun to fade. Feelings of intense loneliness, emptiness or despair are not unusual. Depression can last for days or weeks at a time, and like other feelings it

91

can recur unexpectedly. Usually depression fades gradually of its own accord but it can take time. Talking about your feelings can help. It may also help if you can build into your routine a way to take your mind off how you're feeling, even if only for an hour or two.

## Getting well again

> ### Sandra
>
> 'Even after a year it's as if there are still bubbles of grief inside you. Every now and then one rises to the surface and goes pop – often when you least expect it. As time goes by the bubbles gradually get smaller and fewer.'

In her book *Facing Death*, Averil Stedeford talks about 'grief work' to describe the process of coming to terms with the loss of someone you were close to and becoming emotionally whole again. She illustrates this process with a helpful diagram which is adapted here:

Over time, two people gradually adjust to each other and become attached in a close relationship so that they fit neatly together.

When one person dies, the other is left in a painful shape, with raw surfaces.

Grief work is the process of becoming a rounded person again – taking in some of the characteristics of the person who has died, perhaps taking on roles or learning to do things that you depended on the other person for.

This process of healing may take months – for some people it can take up to two years to begin to feel well again. But at some point you will find yourself beginning to enjoy doing things again for their own sake, not just because you feel you ought to or because other people think it will do you good.

Give yourself plenty of time to pick up the pieces of your own life again, and take things slowly. Caring may have taken over your life for some time, and it may be hard to get used to having only yourself to think about. Sometimes it can help just to talk to someone who knows how you are feeling.

# Help when grief goes wrong

Sometimes grief can get 'stuck'. If you feel unable to start picking up the pieces of your life again, it is important to get help. If you are feeling very depressed, or if the intense feelings of the first days after the death are not beginning to fade, even after some time, it may help to talk to a bereavement counsellor. Your GP, a Macmillan nurse, or a hospice or home care team social worker may be able to offer you counselling themselves, or put you in touch with someone.

If you are severely depressed, your GP may refer you to the community psychiatric nurse or put you in touch with a psychotherapist or psychiatrist. Or you could contact the National Association of Bereavement Services (address on p 104). MIND (address on p 103) also offers – and advises about – counselling and psychotherapy.

## For more *i*nformation

*ⓘ* *Bereavement*, a short leaflet produced by the Royal College of Psychiatrists. Explains the grieving process and gives you advice about how to get help.

*ⓘ* *Through Grief* by Elizabeth Collick, a book about bereavement available from CRUSE (address on p 100).

*i* *Understanding Bereavement*, an advice leaflet available from MIND Publications (address on p 103).

*i* CRUSE – Bereavement Care (address on p 100) is an organisation which helps bereaved people. It has local branches in some areas. Phone the national office or look in your local telephone directory.

*i* **Compassionate Friends** (address on p 99) offers support if you have lost a child of any age.

*i* **The Lesbian and Gay Bereavement Project** (address on p 103) offers support if you have lost a partner or your friend or relative has died of AIDS.

# Useful addresses

**Accountant of Court**
*Information about curator bonis in Scotland*

2 Parliament House
Parliament Square
Edinburgh EH1 1RQ
Tel: 0131-225 2595

**AIDS helplines**
Freephone:
0800 567 123 (English – 24 hours)
0800 555 777 (leaflets and booklets – 24 hours)
0800 282 446 (Cantonese – Tuesday 6–10pm)
0800 282 445 (Punjabi, Bengali, Hindi, Urdu, Gujarati
Wednesday 6–10pm)
0800 282 447 (Arabic – Wednesday 6–10pm)
0800 521 361 (Minicom service for deaf people
daily 10am–10pm)

**Alzheimer Scotland –
Action on Dementia**
*For people caring for someone with dementia who live in Scotland. 24-hour Helpline for people with dementia and their carers in Scotland*

22 Drumsheugh Gardens
Edinburgh EH3 7RN
Tel: 0131-243 1453
Helpline: 0800 317 817

**Alzheimer's Disease Society**
*Information, support and advice about caring for someone with Alzheimer's disease.*

Gordon House
10 Greencoat Place
London SW1P 1PH
Tel: 0171-306 0606

**Asian Family Counselling Service**
*Offers individual and marital counselling service; also bereavement counselling*

6a South Road
Southall
Middlesex UB1 1RT
Tel: 0181-813 8321

**Association of Crossroads Care Attendant Schemes**
*See* Crossroads Care

**BACUP (British Association of Cancer United Patients)**
*Support and information for cancer sufferers and their families. Freephone advice line for people outside London: 0800 181 199.*

3 Bath Place
Rivington Street
London EC2A 3JR
Tel: 0171-696 9003

**Body Positive**
*Helpline for people affected by HIV: 0800 616 212.*

51b Philbeach Garden
Earls Court
London SW5 9EB
Tel: 0171-835 1045

**Breast Cancer Care (BCMA)**
*A free service offering practical advice, information and support to women concerned about breast cancer.*

Kiln House
210 New Kings Road
London SW6 4NZ
Helpline: 0171-384 2344
Freephone:
0500 245 345

**British Association for Counselling**
*To find out about counselling services in your area.*

1 Regent Place
Rugby
Warwickshire CV21 2PJ
Tel: 01788 578328/9

**British Colostomy Association**
*Help, support and advice (not medical advice) for anyone who has a colostomy.*

15 Station Road
Reading
Berkshire RG1 1LG
Tel: 01734 391537

**British Heart Foundation**
*Information about all aspects of heart disease.*

14 Fitzhardinge Street
London W1H 4DH
Tel: 0171-935 0185

**British Holistic Medical Association**
*Publishes self-help books and tapes on a range of subjects including breathing and relaxation, meditation and diet.*

Rowland Thomas House
Royal Shrewsbury Hospital South
Shrewsbury SY3 8XF
Tel: 01743 261155

96

**British Humanist Association**
*For someone to conduct a*
*non-religious funeral ceremony or*
*a form of words you can use.*

47 Theobald's Road
London WC1X 8SP
Tel: 0171-430 0908

**British Institute of Funeral**
**Directors**
*Information about arranging a*
*funeral and about funeral directors*
*in your area.*

140 Leamington Road
Coventry CV3 6JY
Tel: 01203 697160

**British Lung Foundation**
*Information about all aspects of*
*lung disease.*

78 Hatton Garden
London EC1N 8JR
Tel: 0171-831 5831

**British Red Cross**
*Can loan home aids for disabled*
*people. Local branches.*

9 Grosvenor Crescent
London SW1X 7EJ
Tel: 0171-235 5454

**Buddhist Hospice Trust**
*Emotional support and spiritual*
*help for the dying and bereaved.*
*Phone to request a Buddhist*
*volunteer who will visit dying and*
*bereaved people.*

5 Grayswood
Norley Vale
Roehampton
London SW15 4BT
Tel: 0171-789 6170

**Calibre**
*Free cassette library for blind people.*

Aylesbury
Buckingham HP22 5XQ
Tel: 01296 432339/81211

**CALL (Cancer Aid and**
**Listening Line)**
*Support and information for cancer*
*patients and their families. Also has*
*drop-in centres and volunteer*
*support in the Manchester and*
*Stockport areas.*

Swan Buildings
20 Swan Street
Manchester M4 5JW
Tel: 0161-834 6551
24-hour helpline:
0161-835 2586

**Cancer Care Society (CARE)**
*Emotional support and practical*
*help through support groups round*
*the country. Telephone and one-to-one*
*counselling; holiday accommodation.*

21 Zetland Road
Redland
Bristol BD6 7AH
Tel: 0117 94227419

**97**

**Cancer Help Centre**
*Holistic healing programmes to
complement medical treatment:
day courses, residential courses
and follow-up days.*

Grove House
Cornwallis Grove
Clifton
Bristol BS8 4PG
Tel: 0117 9809505

**Cancer Relief Macmillan Fund**
*Can put you in touch with
Macmillan nurse service in your
area.*

Anchor House
15–19 Britten Street
London SW3 3TZ
Tel: 0171-351 7811

**CancerLink**
*Information and advice about all
aspects of cancer.*

11–21 Northdown Street
London N1 9BN
Tel: 0171-833 2818
Freephone information:
0800 132905
Asian freephone:
0800 590415

**Carers National Association**
*Information and advice if you are
caring for someone. Can put you in
touch with other carers and carers'
groups in your area.*

20–25 Glasshouse Yard
London EC1A 4JS
Tel: 0171-490 8818
(1–4pm weekdays)

*London Region:*

5 Chalton Street
London NW1 1JD
Tel: 0171-383 3460

*Scotland:*

3rd Floor
162 Buchanan Street
Glasgow G1 2LL
Tel: 0141-333 9495

*North of England:*

Humphrey Booth Institute
Ladywell Hospital
Eccles New Road
Salford M5 2AA
Tel: 0161-707 8600

**Chest, Heart and Stroke Association**
*See* Stroke Association, British Heart
Foundation and British Lung Foundation.

**Chest, Heart and Stroke Scotland**
*Aims to improve the quality of
life for people in Scotland affected by
chest, heart or stroke illness through
medical research, health promotion,
advice and information, and the
provision of services.*

65 North Castle Street
Edinburgh EH2 3LT
Tel: 0131-225 6963

**Citizens Advice Bureau**
*For advice on legal, financial and
consumer matters. A good place to
turn to if you don't know where to
go for help or advice on any subject.*

Listed in local telephone
directories, or in the
*Yellow Pages* under
'Counselling and advice'.
Other local advice centres
may also be listed.

**Coloplast Foundation**
*Help and advice for people
who have had a colostomy.*

Coloplast Advisory Service
FREEPOST
Peterborough Business
   Park
Peterborough PE2 6BR
Freephone: 0800 622 124
Stoma Care Freephone:
0800 220 622

**Community Care Group
King's Fund Centre**
*Works to improve health and
social care services for the benefit
of the people who need and use them.*

11–15 Cavendish Square
London W1 0AN
Tel: 0171-307 2400

**Community Health Council/
Health Council**
*For enquiries or complaints about
any aspect of the NHS in your area.*

See the local telephone
directory for your area
(sometimes listed under
Health Authority)

**Compassionate Friends**
*A self-help group for parents who
have lost a son or daughter of
any age.*

53 North Street
Bristol BS3 1EN
Tel: 0117 953 9639

**Consumers' Association**
*Publishes regular reports and
full-length books on many
different goods and services.*

2 Marylebone Road
London NW1 4DF
Tel: 0171-486 5544

**99**

**Continence Foundation**
*Advice and information about
whom to contact with incontinence
problems.*

The Basement
2 Doughty Street
London WC1N 2PH
Tel: 0171-404 6875

**Counsel and Care**
*Advice for elderly people and
their families; can sometimes give
grants to help people remain at
home or return to their home.*

Lower Ground Floor
Twyman House
16 Bonny Street
London NW1 9PG
Tel: 0171-485 1566

**Court of Protection**
*If you need to take over the
affairs of someone who is
mentally incapable in England or
Wales.*

Public Trust Office
Protection Division
Stewart House
24 Kingsway
London WC2B 6JX
Tel: 0171-664 7300

**Crossroads Care**
*For a care attendant to come into
your home and look after your
relative.*

10 Regent Place
Rugby
Warwickshire CV21 2PN
Tel: 01788 573653

**CRUSE – Bereavement Care**
*Comfort in bereavement. Can put
you in touch with people in your
area.*

126 Sheen Road
Surrey TW9 1UR
Tel: 0181-940 4818/9047

**Disability Alliance Education
and Research Association**
*Campaigning for a better deal for
people with disabilities;
information about welfare benefits.*

1st Floor East
Universal House
88–94 Wentworth Street
London E1 7SA
Tel: 0171-247 8776
Welfare rights enquiries:
0171-247 8763

**Disability Law Service**
*Free legal advice for disabled
people and their families.*

Room 241
2nd Floor
49–51 Bedford Row
London WC1R 4LR
Tel: 0171-831 8031

**Disabled Living Foundation**
*Information about aids to help
you cope with a disability.*

380–384 Harrow Road
London W9 2HU
Tel: 0171-289 6111

100

**Disability Scotland**
*National organisation for
information on all non-medical
aspects of disability.*

Princes House
5 Shandwick Place
Edinburgh EH2 4RG
Tel: 0131-229 8632
(voice and textphone)

**Elderly Accommodation Council**
*Computerised information about
all forms of accommodation for
older people, including nursing
homes and hospices, and advice
on top-up funding.*

46a Chiswick High Road
London W4 1SZ
Tel: 0181-995 8320/
742 1182

**Health Services Authority**
*The body responsible for GPs and
primary health care.*

See your local telephone
directory.

**Federation of Recruitment
and Employment Services**
*An association of employment
agencies. Send an sae for a list
of agencies in the Nurses and
Carers section and a copy of their
code of good practice.*

36–38 Mortimer Street
London WIN 7RB
Tel: 0171-323 4300

**Forces Help Society**
*Now merged with SSAFA, see p 106.*

**Headway (National Head
Injuries Association)**
*For people who are disabled
physically or mentally as a result
of a head injury, and their carers.*

7 King Edward Court
King Edward Street
Nottingham NG1 1EW
Tel: 0115 912 1000

**Help the Aged**
*Advice and information for
older people and their families.*

16–18 St James's Walk
London EC1R 0BE
Tel: 0171-253 0253
Winter Warmth Hotline/
Seniorline: 0800 650 065

**Hodgkin's Disease Association**
*Information and emotional
support for lymphoma patients
and their families.*

PO Box 275
Haddenham
Aylesbury
Bucks HP17 8JJ
Tel: 01844 291500

**Holiday Care Service**
*Free information and advice
about holidays for elderly or
disabled people and their carers.*

2nd Floor
Imperial Buildings
Victoria Road
Horley
Surrey RH6 7PZ
Tel: 01293 774535

**Hospice Information Service**
*Information about local hospices
which care for people who are
terminally ill.*

St Christopher's Hospice
51–59 Lawrie Park Road
Sydenham
London SE26 6DZ
Tel: 0181-778 9252

**Hysterectomy Support**
*Refers women and families and
partners to former patients for
informal advice and support.
Offers membership of local
support groups.*

c/o Women's Health
52 Featherstone Street
London EC1Y 8RT
Tel: 0171-251 6580
(10am–4pm Mon,
Wed–Fri)

**Incontinence Information
Helpline**
*Information and advice about
managing incontinence, and how to
contact your nearest continence adviser.*

Tel: 0191-213 0050

**Institute for Complementary
Medicine**
*Provides names of practitioners on
the British Register of Complementary
Practitioners. Send large sae stating
area of interest, eg homeopathy,
osteopathy, massage, etc.*

PO Box 194
London SE16 1QZ

**Institute of Family Therapy**
*Family therapy for recently
bereaved families or those with
seriously ill members. Services
free but donations welcome.*

24–32 Stephenson Way
London NW1 2HX
Tel: 0171-391 9150

**Jewish Care**
*Social care, personal support,
residential homes for Jewish people.*

Stuart Young House
221 Golders Green Road
London NW11 9DQ
Tel: 0181-458 3282

**Lesbian and Gay Bereavement Project**
*Counselling, support and advice for gay men, lesbians, and their friends and families.*

Vaughan M Williams Centre
Colindale Hospital
London NW9 5HG
Tel: 0181-200 0511
(3–6pm weekdays)
Helpline: 0181-455 8894
(7pm–midnight)

**Leukaemia Care Society**
*Promotes the welfare of people with leukaemia and allied blood disorders.*

14 Kingfisher Court
Vennybridge
Exeter EX1 8JN
Tel: 01392 464848

**Marriage Counselling Scotland**
*Counselling and help with difficult relationships.*

105 Hanover Street
Edinburgh EH2 1DJ
Tel: 0131-225 5006

**Marie Curie Cancer Care**
*Nursing care and advice for cancer patients.*

28 Belgrave Square
London SW1X 8QG
Tel: 0171-235 3325

**MIND (National Association for Mental Health)**
*Information, support and publications about all aspects of mental illness, depression, etc.*

Granta House
15–19 The Broadway
London E15 4BQ
Tel: 0181-519 2122

**MIND Publications Mail Order Service**

See address above.

**Motor Neurone Disease Association**
*Advice, information leaflets and an equipment loan service. Makes financial grants to people with motor neurone disease to help with care.*

PO Box 246
Northampton NN1 2PR
Tel: 01604 250505
Helpline for patients and carers: 01345 626262

**Multiple Sclerosis Society of Great Britain and Northern Ireland**
*Provides a welfare support service for the families of people with multiple sclerosis.*

25 Effie Road
London SW6 1EE
Tel: 0171-736 6267
Helpline: 0171-371 8000
(10am–4pm)

**National Association of
Bereavement Services**
*Information about bereavement
counselling services in your area.*

20 Norton Folgate
London E1 6DB
Tel: 0171-247 1080
(24-hour answerphone)

**National Association of Funeral
Directors**
*Offers code of conduct and a
simple service for a basic funeral.*

618 Warwick Road
Solihull B91 1AA
Tel: 0121-711 1343

**National Association of
Laryngectomee Clubs**
*Runs clubs which provide speech
therapy, social support and
monthly meetings. Advises on
speech aids and medical supplies.*

Ground Floor
6 Rickett Street
Fulham
London SW6 1RU
Tel: 0171-381 9993

**National Care Homes Association**
*An umbrella body for local
associations of private care homes;
can put you in touch with homes
in your area, and give you advice.*

3rd Floor
Martin House
84–86 Gray's Inn Road
London WC1X 8BQ
Tel: 0171-915 3120

**National Council for Hospice and
Specialist Palliative Care Services**
*Provides advice and facilitates the
sharing of knowledge, information
and experience.*

Heron House
322 High Holborn
London WC1V 7PW
Tel: 0171-269 4550

**National Head Injuries Association**
*See* Headway

**National Secular Society**
*For someone to conduct a
non-religious ceremony or a form of
words you can use.*

47 Theobald's Road
London WC1X 8SP
Tel: 0171-404 3126

**Natural Death Centre**
*Helps families arrange funerals
without undertakers. If writing for
information please send an sae.*

20 Heber Road
London NW2 6AA
Tel: 0181-208 2853

**Neuroblastoma Society**
*Information and advice by
telephone or letter for patients and
their families.*

41 Towncourt Crescent
Pettswood
Kent BR5 1PH
Tel: 01689 873338

104

**Oesophageal Patients' Association**
*Leaflets, telephone advice and*
*support, before and during treatment.*
*Visits, where possible, by former*
*patients with oesophageal cancer.*

16 Whitefields Crescent
Solihull
West Midlands
B91 3NU
Tel: 0121-704 9860

**Parkinson's Disease Society**
*Information and advice for people*
*caring for someone with Parkinson's*
*disease; many local branches.*

22 Upper Woburn Place
London WC1H 0RA
Tel: 0171-383 3513

**Pensions Advisory Service**
*For queries and problems to do*
*with occupational pensions.*

11 Belgrave Road
London SW1V 1RB
Tel: 0171-233 8080

**RADAR (Royal Association for**
**Disability and Rehabilitation)**

Unit 12 City Forum
250 City Road
London EC1V 0AF
Tel: 0171-250 3222

**Registered Nursing Home**
**Association**
*Information about registered*
*private nursing homes in your area.*

Calthorpe House
Hagley Road
Edgbaston
Birmingham B16 8QY
Tel: 0121-454 2511

**Relate (formerly National Marriage**
**Guidance Council)**
*Counselling and help with difficult*
*relationships; many local branches.*

Herbert Gray College
Little Church Street
Rugby
Warwickshire CV21 3AP
Tel: 01788 573241/
560811

**Relatives Association**
*Support and advice for the relatives*
*of people in a residential or nursing*
*home or in hospital long-term.*

5 Tavistock Place
London WC1H 9SS
Tel: 0171-916 6055/
0181-201 9153

**Retinoblastoma Society**
*Links families to give moral support*
*and practical help. Enables parents*
*to exchange information and share*
*experiences.*

c/o Academic Department
of Paediatric Oncology
St Bartholomew's Hospital
West Smithfield
London EC1A 7BE
Tel: 0171-600 3309

**Samaritans**
*Someone to talk to if you are in despair.*

See your local telephone directory.

**Save our Sons (SOS)**
*Information and emotional support for men and boys with testicular cancer.*

Shirley Wilcox
Tides Reach
1 Kite Hill
Wooton Bridge
Isle of Wight PO33 4LA
Tel: 0983 882876
(evenings preferred)

**Scottish Council for Voluntary Organisations**
*For information about voluntary organisations in Scotland*

18–19 Claremont Crescent
Edinburgh EH7 4QD
Tel: 0131-556 3882

**Self–help Centre**
*A voluntary organisation that has a database of local and national groups for specific illnesses and disabilities.*

Regent's Wharf
8 All Saints Street
London N1 9RL
Tel: 0171-713 6161

**Soldiers, Sailors and Airmen Family Association (SSAFA)**
*Help for service or ex-service men and women and their families.*

19 Queen Elizabeth Street
London SE1 2LP
Tel: 0171-403 8783/
0171-962 9696

**Spinal Injuries Association**
*Information and advice for people who are disabled as a result of spinal injury.*

Newpoint House
76 St James's Lane
London N10 3DF
Tel: 0181-444 2121

**SPOD (Association to Aid the Sexual and Personal Relationships of People with a Disability)**
*Telephone counselling Monday and Wednesday 1.30–4.30pm;Tuesday and Thursday 10.30am–1.30pm.*

286 Camden Road
London N7 OBJ
Tel: 0171-607 8851

**Standing Conference of Ethnic Minority Senior Citizens**
*Information, support and advice for older people from ethnic minorities and their families.*

5 Westminster Bridge Road
London SE1 7XW
Tel: 0171-928 0095

**Stroke Association**
*Information and advice if you are caring for someone who has had a stroke.*

123–127 Whitecross Street
London EC1Y 8JJ
Tel: 0171-490 7999
(1.00–3.55pm)

**Sue Ryder Foundation**
*Six Sue Ryder Homes in England specialise in cancer care. Visiting nurses care for patients in their own homes. Advice and bereavement counselling*

Sue Ryder Homes
Cavendish
Sudbury
Suffolk CO10 8AY
Tel: 01787 280252

**Tak Tent**
*Gives emotional support, counselling and information on cancers and treatments.*

Cancer Support
 Organisation
G Block
Western Infirmary
Glasgow G11 6NT
Tel: 0141-211 1930

**Tenovus**
*Emotional support and information on all aspects of cancer. Helpline answered by cancer-trained nurses and counsellors; available to everyone, but provides comprehensive bilingual service for the people of Wales.*

Cancer Information Centre
PO Box 88
College Buildings
Courtney Road
Splott
Cardiff CF1 1SA
Tel: 01222 497700
Helpline: 0800 526 527

**Terrence Higgins Trust**
*Information and advice about HIV/AIDS.*

52–54 Gray's Inn Road
London WC1X 8JU
Tel: 0171-831 0330
Helpline: 0171-242 1010
(12–10pm daily)

**Tripscope**
*For free information and advice about travel and transport for disabled and older people.*

The Courtyard
Evelyn Road
London W4 5JL
Tel/Textphone:
0345 585641

**Ulster Cancer Foundation**
*Cancer information helpline;*
*information and resource centre;*
*rehabilitation programmes and*
*support groups for patients and*
*relatives.*

40–42 Eglantine Avenue
Belfast BT9 6DX
Tel: 01232 663281/2/3
Helpline: 01232 663439
(9.30am–12.30pm
weekdays)

**United Kingdom Home Care**
**Association (UKHCA)**
*For information about organisations*
*providing home care in your area.*

42B Banstead Road
Carshalton
Surrey SM5 3NW
Tel: 0181-288 1551

**Wales Council for Voluntary Action**
*Information about voluntary groups*
*in Wales.*

Llys Ifor
Crescent Road
Caerphilly
Mid Glamorgan CF8 1XL
Tel: 01222 869224/86911

**Women's Royal Voluntary Service**
*Provides meals at home for ill and*
*disabled people in some areas.*

Milton Hill House
Milton Hill
Oxfordshire OX13 6AF
Tel: 01235 442917

# About Age Concern

**Caring for someone who is dying** is one of a wide range of publications produced by Age Concern England, the National Council on Ageing. Age Concern cares about all older people and believes later life should be fulfilling and enjoyable. For too many this is impossible. As the leading charitable movement in the UK concerned with ageing and older people, Age Concern finds effective ways to change that situation.

Where possible, we enable older people to solve problems themselves, providing as much or as little support as they need. Our network of 1,400 local groups, supported by 250,000 volunteers, provides community-based services such as lunch clubs, day centres and home visiting.

Nationally, we take a lead role campaigning, parliamentary work, policy analysis, research, specialist information and advice provision, and publishing. Innovative programmes promote healthier lifestyles and provide older people with opportunities to give the experience of a lifetime back to their communities.

Age Concern is dependent on donations, covenants and legacies.

**Age Concern England**
1268 London Road
London SW16 4ER
Tel: 0181-679 8000

**Age Concern Scotland**
113 Rose Street
Edinburgh EH2 3DT
Tel: 0131-220 3345

**Age Concern Cymru**
4th Floor
1 Cathedral Road
Cardiff CF1 9SD
Tel: 01222 371566

**Age Concern Northern Ireland**
3 Lower Crescent
Belfast BT7 1NR
Tel: 01232 245729

# Other books in this series

**The Carer's Handbook: What to do and who to turn to**
*Marina Lewycka*
At some point in their lives millions of people find themselves suddenly responsible for organising the care of an older person with a health crisis. All too often such carers have no idea what services are available or who can be approached for support. This book is designed to act as a first point of reference in just such an emergency, signposting readers on to many more detailed, local sources of advice.
£6.99 0–86242–262–0

**Finding and paying for residential and nursing home care**
*Marina Lewycka*
Acknowledging that an older person needs residential care often represents a major crisis for family and friends. Feelings of guilt and betrayal invariably compound the difficulties faced in identifying a suitable care home and sorting out the financial arrangements. This book provides a practical step-by-step guide to the decisions which have to be made and the help available.
£6.99 0–86242–261–2

For details of these or the other titles making up the series, please contact the Publishing Department for a Books Catalogue.

# Publications from Age Concern Books

## Money matters

### Your Rights: A guide to money benefits for older people
*Sally West*
A highly acclaimed annual guide to the State benefits available to older people. Contains current information on Income Support, Housing Benefit, Council Tax Benefit and retirement pensions, among other sources of financial help, and includes advice on how to claim them.
For further information please telephone 0181-679 8000.

### Your Taxes and Savings: A guide for older people
*Sally West and Money Management Council*
This annual publication explains how the tax system affects older people and offers advice on how to avoid paying more tax than necessary. The savings information covers the wide range of investment opportunities now available and includes advice on building up a portfolio. Guidance is also given on budgeting and managing retirement income.
For further information please telephone 0181-679 8000.

### The Pensions Handbook: The pensions system explained
*Sue Ward*
Many older people in their later working lives become concerned about the adequacy of their existing pension arrangements. This title addresses these worries and suggests strategies via which the value of a prospective pension can be enhanced. Advice is also provided on monitoring company pension schemes.
For further information please telephone 0181-679 8000.

### Managing Other People's Money
*Penny Letts*
The management of money and property is usually a personal and private matter. However, there may come a time when someone else has to take over on either a temporary or a permanent basis. This book looks at the circumstances in which such a need could arise and provides a step-by-step guide to the arrangements which have to be made.
£9.99 0–86242–250–7

## Health and care

### CareFully: A guide for home care assistants
*Lesley Bell*
Recent legislation places increasing emphasis on the delivery of care to older people in their own homes, thereby underlining the crucial role of home care assistants. This accessible guide provides practical advice on the day-to-day tasks encountered and addresses such issues as legal responsibilities and emotional involvement.
£11.99 0–86242–129–2

### Living, Loving and Ageing: Sexual and personal relationships in later life
*Wendy Greengross and Sally Greengross*
Sexuality is often regarded as the preserve of the younger generation. This book, for older people and those who work with them, tackles the issues in a straightforward fashion, avoiding preconceptions and bias.
£5.99 0–86242–070–9

## General

### Eating Well on a Budget
*Sara Lewis*
Completely revised, the new edition of this successful title offers sound advice on shopping and cooking cost-effectively and includes wholesome original recipes for four complete weekly menus.
£4.66 0–86242–120–9

## The Retirement Handbook 2nd Edition
*Caroline Hartnell*

Some people eagerly look forward to retirement, some dread it; most people probably fall somewhere between the two. Whatever your attitude, however positive your feelings, retirement is a time of adjustment – and adjustment is not always easy.

A comprehensive handbook for people on the point of retirement, this book is packed full of practical information and advice on all the opportunities available. Drawing on Age Concern's wealth of experience, it covers everything you need to know, including:

- managing your money
- staying healthy
- using your time
- housing options

*The Retirement Handbook* is designed to encourage everyone to view retirement as an opportunity not to be missed. Positive and upbeat, reading this book will make you wonder how you had time for work!

£7.99 0–86242–237–X

---

If you would like to order any of these titles, please write to the address below, enclosing a cheque or money order for the appropriate amount made payable to Age Concern England. Credit card orders may be made on 0181-679 8000.

**Mail Order Unit**
Age Concern England
1268 London Road
London SW16 4ER

---

# Factsheets from Age Concern

Covering many areas of concern to older people, Age Concern's factsheets are comprehensive and totally up to date. There are over 40 factsheets, with each one providing straightforward information and impartial advice in a simple and easy-to-use format. Topics covered include:

- finding and paying for residential and nursing home care
- raising income from your home
- money benefits
- legal arrangements for managing financial affairs
- finding help at home

Single copies are available free on receipt of a 9" × 12" sae.

Age Concern offers a factsheet subscription service which presents all the factsheets in a folder, together with regular updates throughout the year. The first year's subscription currently costs £40; an annual renewal thereafter is £20.

---

For further information, or to order factsheets, write to:

**Information and Policy Division**
Age Concern England
1268 London Road
London SW16 4ER

---

For readers in Scotland wishing further information, or to order factsheets, please write to:

Age Concern Scotland
113 Rose Street
Edinburgh EH2 3DT

Subscribers in Scotland will automatically be sent Scottish editions of factsheets where law and practice differ in Scotland.

# Index